DEFENCE OF THE REALM

DEFENCE

OF THE

REALM

———◆———

ALUN CHALFONT

COLLINS
8 Grafton Street, London W1
1987

William Collins Sons & Co. Ltd
London · Glasgow · Sydney · Auckland
Toronto · Johannesburg

BRITISH LIBRARY CATALOGUING IN PUBLICATION DATA

Chalfont, Alun Jones, *Baron*
Defence of the realm.
1. Great Britain—Military policy
I. Title
355'.0335'41   UA647

ISBN 0-00-217980-6

First published in 1987
Copyright © Alun Chalfont 1987

Set in Monophoto Ehrhardt by
Ace Filmsetting Ltd, Frome, Somerset
Printed and Bound in Great Britain by
T.J. Press (Padstow) Ltd, Padstow, Cornwall

For Mona

CONTENTS

'Once we cut expenditure to the extent where our security is imperilled, we have no houses, we have no hospitals, we have no schools, we have a heap of cinders.'

Denis Healey, Secretary of State for Defence, House of Commons, March 1969

PREFACE

This book has been written with one primary aim: to provide a comprehensible background to an issue on which there is virtually no common ground among this country's political parties – national defence.

It is divided into three main sections. First, an analysis of what threatens the survival of free, democratic societies. This section contains source material for anyone setting out to understand the nature of the threat, which is still not widely or clearly recognized. It draws extensively on Soviet sources.

The second section considers the global context against which the principal threat must be assessed. It identifies the main pressure points in the structure of international relations and underlines the limitations of a post-imperial power in the management of global crises.

Part Three is an assessment of Britain's role and responsibilities in a rapidly changing strategic environment. It argues the importance of a nuclear deterrent in the foreign and military policies of the United Kingdom, but it concludes that strong conventional forces are also essential in a comprehensive and effective defence policy.

Strategy in the age of nuclear weapons and advanced military technology is a profoundly complicated issue. The debate among experts is often conducted in a language as specialized as that of medicine or linguistic philosophy. The vocabulary of arms control and nuclear strategy can be an impenetrable thicket of jargon. Familiarity with the jargon is not essential to an understanding of the fundamental issues of defence policy, and in this book I have made every effort to avoid it. There are, however, a few basic terms and concepts with which it is necessary to become acquainted if the argument is to be understood.

One of the most persistent sources of misunderstanding is the confusion between a 'first strike' and the 'first use' of nuclear weapons.

'First strike' denotes the use by one nuclear power of nuclear weapons designed to destroy the nuclear delivery systems of another nuclear power in order to remove his ability to retaliate. A first strike can be launched with or without a conventional attack.

'First use' signifies the use by a nation or alliance of its nuclear weapons in response to a purely conventional attack. The threat of 'first use' is designed to deter an enemy from launching such an attack.

Missiles, weapons, warheads, launchers and delivery systems are another semantic jungle. A delivery system is any platform used to launch nuclear missiles. The delivery system can be ground-based, submarine-based, seaborne or airborne. The missile may be ballistic, which means that it is fired into space like a bullet, to follow a predictable trajectory before returning to earth; or it may be non-ballistic, or 'air-breathing', which means that it travels through the atmosphere like an aircraft.

The range of missiles is usually described as intercontinental (ICBM); intermediate-range, between 300 and 1200 miles (IRBM); or shorter range. Shorter range missiles are sometimes referred to as 'battlefield' nuclear weapons.

A missile may carry one or more nuclear warheads. If these are multiple warheads, they separate from the main missile during its flight. They then fall to their targets either on a predictable ballistic trajectory, when they are known as multiple re-entry vehicles (MRVs); or guided by computers on to separate targets, when they are known as multiple independently targeted re-entry vehicles (MIRVs).

The 'yield' of a warhead denotes its explosive power, expressed in terms of its equivalent in conventional high explosive. Thus a ten-kiloton warhead explodes with the power of 10,000 tons of high explosive; a megaton warhead with the power of a million tons, and so on.

If, even with the assistance of this brief and selective glossary of the more frequently used terms in the strategic debate, the reader is still confused, then I have failed in my purpose and I can only fall back on the ultimate escape clause – anyone who says he is *not* confused by nuclear strategy should be treated with the utmost suspicion.

Much of the material in this study has previously appeared, in different forms, in various journals and reports, and I have thought it useful to publish it in the form of a short book at a time when national defence is a matter of great public concern. I would like to acknowledge my debt to: Mr Ian Greig, whose compilation of quotations from Soviet authorities, *They Mean What They Say* (Foreign Affairs Research Institute, London, 1981), is invaluable source material; Dr G. A. Keyworth II, former Science Adviser to President Reagan, for his advice and guidance on the Strategic Defence Initiative; and Mr Herbert Meyer, for special insights into the situation in Central America.

I am grateful to Mr Robert Hannigan for some diligent and imaginative research; and to the staff of the Library of the House of Lords for unfailing courtesy and help; and to Camilla Brace for services at the word-processor above and beyond the call of duty.

The modest hope which lies behind this book is that it will give aid and comfort to people in this country who still believe that the most important task of any government is to ensure that those whom it governs are kept safe from present dangers.

INTRODUCTION

The landscape of international relations is being radically transformed. Some familiar signposts are beginning to disappear, or at least to become indistinct. The world is an increasingly uncertain place, and it is important that those who live in it should understand something of the volatile international scene upon which their government is required to perform.

The West is, to put it bluntly, in a mess. The American presidency is once again under siege by a coalition of political opportunists and investigative journalists who can never quite forget the intoxicating experience of Watergate, together with a number of well-disposed people who believe, with some justification, that President Reagan has been guilty of serious errors of judgment. One of the results of this has been an intensification in Washington of the search for some dramatic success in foreign policy designed to restore the Reagan magic.

This has been concentrated, predictably, on the field of arms control. Already the Reagan strategy of 'hanging tough' on the Strategic Defence Initiative has paid its first dividend. Mr Gorbachev has proposed an agreement on intermediate-range missiles in Europe which is for all practical purposes the 'zero option' already put forward by the United States. If, in the course of serious negotiation, the two sides can resolve the problems of verification, come to an agreement on short-range nuclear missiles, and ensure that the Russian SS20s are not simply moved to the other end of the Sverdlovsk–Berlin highway, they might achieve a serious arms control treaty.

One of the consequences of this, however, is that the United States is likely to be increasingly prepared to negotiate such agreements with the Soviet Union based upon a perception of superpower interests, with the concerns of Western Europe assuming a much lower priority. Already there are signs that the security of the European–Atlantic area may no longer be uppermost in the minds of American strategic planners. The emergence of a communist threat in Central America, together with the gradual shift in the geopolitical and economic centre of gravity to the Pacific Basin, is causing Americans, already frustrated by the inability of Western Europe to 'get its act together' and irritated by the anti-Americanism of the European left, to question the value of their military commitment to their 'entangling alliance'.

This somewhat disturbing scenario indicates clearly the kind of defence policy which Britain will need as it moves into the 1990s. One of its important duties will be to play a leading role in the restoration of a sense of unity and purpose in Western Europe. The 'European idea' has all but collapsed in a muddle of short-sighted nationalism. There is no common military strategy, no effective harmonization of foreign policy and no shared sense of the dangers which lie ahead. Britain can, and should, take a lead in putting this right.

One of the primary aims of a coordinated European foreign policy should be to ensure the continued commitment of the United States to the solidarity of NATO and to the security of the European–Atlantic area. This will require a clearer recognition by European leaders that the United States has legitimate security concerns outside the NATO area. Europe cannot afford the luxury of Yankee-baiting every time the United States seeks to protect its perceived interests, even if it sometimes does so in a way which meets with fastidious disapproval in the sophisticated chancelleries of Paris, London and Bonn.

Western Europe is also faced with the need to take its military defence more seriously than it has shown much sign of doing in the past. The continued presence of a large American army in Europe cannot any longer be taken for granted; nor can the European members of NATO rely permanently on the American nuclear guarantee. Defence cooperation is no longer merely desirable as a catalyst for political unity. It has become an imperative for survival.

This is no time to be playing Russian roulette with national defence policy. It may well be that in the course of the complicated and subtle changes now emerging in the international balance of power, Britain's nuclear deterrent may be an important factor both in the emergence of a European Defence Community and in the arms control equation. To abandon it unilaterally now in obedience to ill-conceived political dogmas would be an act of unparalleled irresponsibility.

PART ONE

—————◆—————

The Present Danger

CHAPTER ONE

The View from the Kremlin

One of the primary functions of any elected government is to ensure the safety of its people and the survival of their free political institutions. Thomas Hobbes, describing in *Leviathan* the duties of a sovereign state 'on whom the Sovereign Power is conferred by the Consent of the People assembled', argued that when men and women invest authority in a government, their sole purpose is to ensure peace and security. This involves the prevention of discord at home and hostility from abroad. The government, therefore, is entrusted with

> . . . the Right of making Warre, and Peace with other nations, and Common-Wealths; that is to say of judging when it is for the publique good, and how great forces are to be assembled, armed and payd for that end; and to levy mony upon the Subjects, to defray the expenses thereof. . . .

Three centuries later, it would be difficult to improve upon Hobbes's analysis of the obligations which a democratic government undertakes in formulating and putting into effect its defence policy.

Before doing so, however, a prudent government must construct some frame of reference. It must proceed from a set of principles and assumptions upon which it can base intelligent policies designed to promote national security, within a stable international order. A fundamental consideration is the role of armed force in relations between nation states. Frederick the Great put it in characteristically robust, if slightly enigmatic, terms. 'Diplomacy without arms', he said, 'is like music without instruments.' Sir Michael Howard, Regius Professor of Modern History at Oxford, has expressed the matter more lucidly: 'International conflict', in his view, 'is an ineluctable product of diversity of interests, perceptions and cultures . . . armed conflict is immanent in any international system.' In other words, although war can often be avoided, or its effects mitigated by patient and realistic statesmanship, it will not be eliminated from the conduct of international affairs simply because it is demonstrably cruel and destructive. Indeed, it would be difficult for anyone not engaged in the business of conjuring up dream-worlds to conceive of a stable international system which would not ultimately rely in some way upon the sanction of force.

Clearly, then, effective arrangements for national security must include adequate military defence against external attack. Before this can be achieved, the threat of any such attack must be identified and evaluated. It seems reasonable to suggest that the principal *external* threat to the integrity of the United Kingdom and the survival of its political institutions comes at present from the Soviet Union. International terrorism, as a form of low-intensity warfare conducted against Western democracies, also poses a security problem of a special kind, and the nature of this threat and the responses to it are analysed in Chapters 4 to 6. It is a phenomenon which has an indirect relevance to national defence policy, although the direct impact of its threat is felt in the context of internal security. There are also military problems posed by threats to stability outside the main confrontation between the Soviet Union and the West. These are considered in Part II. The main criterion on which British defence policy has to be formulated, however, is the threat posed by an aggressive, expansionist Soviet Union, openly committed to the Marxist–Leninist ideology. The new regime of Mr Mikhail Gorbachev has initiated some superficial domestic reforms in the name of *glasnost*, or openness; it may also bring about a measure of efficiency and self-confidence in a Soviet society which has for long been demoralized by a stifling bureaucratic apathy. Mr Gorbachev has, however, said nothing to indicate that he will change to any significant extent the external policies of the Soviet Union, which have been the subject of consistent pronouncements by Soviet leaders for more than half a century.

The export of the communist revolution to the rest of the world is still a central aim of Marxism-Leninism, the doctrine upon which the foreign policy of the Soviet Union remains firmly based. Lenin himself left no doubt about the long-term programme:

> . . . the existence of the Soviet Republic alongside the imperialist states is inconceivable in the long term. In the end one or the other will be victorious and until this end is reached a succession of most terrible clashes between the Soviet Republic and the bourgeois States is unavoidable.[1]

The Soviet Union bases its policy of global expansion on the theory that the decay of capitalism is inevitable and that the USSR has a duty to create the conditions in which this inexorable historical process can take place. In 1972 Leonid Brezhnev wrote:

> The Communist Party of the Soviet Union always held and now holds that the class struggle between the two systems . . . will continue. It cannot be otherwise, because the world outlook and class aims of Socialism and Capitalism are opposed and irreconcilable.[2]

And the position was stated more recently and with even greater clarity by an authoritative Soviet commentator:

> Communists do not conceal the fact that the elimination of the rotten Capitalist system and the building of Socialism on a worldwide scale is their ultimate goal.[3]

Most modern historians accept that the Marxist revolution is conceived as a global phenomenon. The only flexibility lies in the tactical means to be adopted to achieve the ultimate strategic aim. Any means – political, economic or military – are to be used, the only criterion of selection being that which offers the clearest possibility of success at any given time. In the most literal sense it can be said that the USSR has, by its own standards, no *territorial* ambitions. Its ambition is rather the establishment of worldwide communism, generally referred to as 'socialism'. The policy known as the Brezhnev Doctrine envisages the Soviet Union at the centre of a system of states with limited sovereignty, but regarded by the USSR as 'free and independent socialist states'; and Brezhnev himself was reported by *Pravda* as saying in November 1968 that a threat to one country's socialism:

> becomes not only a problem for the people of that country, but also a general problem, the concern of all Socialist countries.[4]

According to this doctrine the Soviet action in Hungary and Czechoslovakia could not be described as an 'invasion', nor could Afghanistan be regarded as a territorial gain.

This interpretation obviously cannot be accepted uncritically. It is often difficult clearly to distinguish between the spread of Soviet communism and territorial expansion. The real logic of the situation is that since the USSR sponsors global communism, its territorial ambitions are unlimited. Gromyko's defence of the invasion of Afghanistan lends some weight to this proposition:

> Lenin's cause lives and triumphs on our planet. The enemies of Leninism vainly try to confine it to certain geographical boundaries: there are no such boundaries. . . .
> Lenin regarded proletarian internationalism as the major principle in the relations between existing Socialism and the international working-class movement, on the one hand, and the national liberation movement on the other. . . . The principle of proletarian internationalism was in action in Ethiopia in the 1930s, in Egypt and Algeria in the 1950s and 1960s, in Angola, Ethiopia and other countries in the 1970s. And the same principle is currently in action in Afghanistan.[5]

The record of the Soviet Union since the Second World War is one of constant expansion and persistent intervention. A Soviet presence, usually including a military element, has been established in Vietnam, Afghanistan, Yemen, the Horn of Africa, Libya, Egypt (from which it was abruptly expelled by President Sadat), Angola, Mozambique and Cuba. The USSR has intervened decisively in East Germany in 1953, Hungary in 1956, Czechoslovakia in 1968 and Poland in 1981, where some thirty Soviet divisions stationed around Poland were swiftly mobilized and brought up to full strength. A Soviet military force of two tank divisions was already positioned in Poland, and that force did not increase in 1981.

However, the clear inference which was to be drawn from the sudden mobilization of an additional thirty divisions on the Polish border was that military force *would* be used if the Polish authorities did not move swiftly to effect a return to order. As a result the USSR was warned by NATO defence ministers and by EEC members, among others, that an invasion of Poland would have grave consequences for East–West relations.[6]

In his report to the Supreme Soviet of the USSR in July 1969, Gromyko declared:

> It is natural . . . that the Soviet Union, which as a major world power has widely developed international ties, cannot react passively even towards events that might be territorially remote but which affect our security and the security of our friends. . . . Our country's influence on world affairs unswervingly increases year by year, and one might say, day by day. . . . Distance cannot weaken the great attractive force of the Soviet Union's foreign policy, nor the strength, as a whole, of the ideas that our Socialist state carries into the outside world.[7]

To support a foreign policy of expansion and intervention, the Soviet Union has built up a massive military force, including more than 5 million men and women under arms and 5 million more trained reserves. The Soviet Navy, which was thirty years ago a relatively small coastal force, is now a powerful ocean-going navy, with fleets permanently deployed in all the oceans of the world, and with an extensive capacity for the distant projection of military force.[8] Much Soviet expansion and intervention is carried out in the form of aid and support to indigenous revolutionary movements. As an editorial in the Moscow *New Times* has put it:

> The history of the revolutionary movement confirms the moral and political rightness of this form of aid and support. . . . To refuse to use the potential which Socialist countries possess

would mean in fact to avoid fulfilling an international duty and returning the world to the times when Imperialism would stifle any revolutionary movement with impunity as it saw fit.[9]

While it professes to be committed to 'democracy' and 'self-determination', its actions clearly demonstrate that the USSR does not regard these as desirable objectives in themselves. Soviet doctrine defines self-determination as determination by socialist regimes, or by revolutionary movements against non-socialist states. It does not include determination by majority will. Where class struggle exists – that is to say, everywhere except in totalitarian communist countries – genuine self-determination would not be included in the objectives of Soviet foreign policy. The case history of Afghanistan demonstrates clearly the attitude of the USSR towards self-determination and democratic rights.

Before the invasion in 1979, the Soviet Union professed respect for the foreign policy of Afghanistan. Indeed, Article 5 of the Soviet–Afghan friendship treaty, signed in December 1978, declared that:

> The Union of Soviet Socialist Republics respects the policy of non-alignment which is pursued by the Democratic Republic of Afghanistan and which is an important factor for maintaining international peace and security.

When, however, this policy of non-alignment became a major irritant to the Soviet Union with the overthrow in 1979 of Nur Mohammed Taraki, President of the Democratic Republic of Afghanistan, who had signed the friendship treaty, preparations for military intervention were put in hand. Nevertheless, as late as 23 December, a few days before the massive airlift of Russian troops, the government-controlled *Pravda* was still playing the self-determination tune:

> Western, and particularly American, mass media have recently been disseminating deliberately inspired rumours about some sort of Soviet 'interference' in Afghanistan's internal affairs. Things have even got as far as allegations that Soviet 'combat units' have been introduced in Afghan territory. All this, of

course, represents the most 'transparent' fabrications – but fabrications with a sinister purpose and which pursue political aims dangerous to the Afghan people.

After the invasion, however, came the predictable justification. Brezhnev declared simply:

> To have acted otherwise would have meant leaving Afghanistan a prey to Imperialism. . . .

The invading force was, of course, to be nothing more than a temporary presence, as Brezhnev went on to say:

> The only task set to the Soviet contingents is to assist the Afghans in repulsing the aggression from outside. They will be fully withdrawn once the causes that made the Afghan leadership request their introduction disappear.[10]

It is interesting to note that similar declarations were made after the invasion of Hungary in 1956:

> when order has been restored in Hungary and its Government considers the presence of Soviet troops is not necessary, the Soviet Union for its part will under no circumstances insist on its forces remaining there.[11]

And of Czechoslovakia in 1968:

> On 21 August Soviet military units . . . entered the territory of Czechoslovakia. They will be immediately withdrawn from the CSR as soon as the threat to Socialism's achievements that has developed in Czechoslovakia, a threat to the security of countries in the Socialist commonwealth, is eliminated and legal authorities find that the further stay of these military units is no longer necessary.[12]

In contrast to the virtual siege of Poland, Soviet troops actually crossed the borders of Hungary in 1956 and Czechoslovakia in 1968.

Hungary already had four divisions of Soviet troops permanently stationed there, and Czechoslovakia similarly had a permanent presence. Despite the assurances that all troops would be withdrawn once order had been restored to both countries, the additional troops, as promised, left; the permanent force has remained to this day.

Apart from periodic tactical changes brought about by the shifting 'correlation of forces', Soviet foreign policy has remained remarkably consistent in its aims, which continue to be conditioned by the view that the fundamental conflict between 'socialism' and capitalism conditions the entire process of world development. To put it another way, the foreign policy of the Soviet Union continues to be based on the Marxist–Leninist doctrine of the inevitability of the revolutionary transition from capitalism to socialism.

Writing in *Izvestia* in 1972, the Soviet commentator Boris Dimitriyev emphasized that there could be no relaxation in this process:

> The Soviet Union invariably and consistently follows Lenin's instructions in the sphere of foreign policy. The Soviet Union's approach to international affairs vividly reflects the fact that USSR foreign policy is a class policy of a socialist state, whose interests are inseparable from the goals of the world workers' and communist movement. . . .
>
> It is futile for anyone to reckon on the Soviet Union's tolerating any relaxation in the ideological sphere or giving up its principles for the sake of short-term advantages. . . .[13]

And in the following year Brezhnev was reported in *Pravda*, underlining the continuity of the process:

> The foundations of our Socialist . . . foreign policy were laid down by the great Lenin. We Soviet Communists see in Lenin's ideas, in the principles he elaborated, a reliable guide.[14]

He and his predecessors appear clearly to have believed that the total triumph of socialism throughout the world is inevitable. There is no evidence to suppose that this view has changed so far as his successors, including the genial Mr Gorbachev, are concerned.

It is difficult in the light of repeated statements by Soviet leaders to believe that the two systems will ever be able to exist peacefully together. 'Peaceful coexistence', like 'detente', is a concept developed by the Soviet Union to denote a phase in the continuing struggle between communism and capitalism. As with many other words and phrases in the specialized language of Marxism-Leninism, its real meaning is very different from that which it appears to be. Just as 'democratic republic' usually denotes a state from which all recognizable forms of democracy have been eliminated, 'peaceful coexistence' means a form of hostility short of armed conflict. The *Great Soviet Encyclopedia*, an authoritative and well-recognized vehicle for the expression of Soviet policy, defines it as:

> a specific form of class struggle between Socialism and Capitalism in the international arena. . . . The basically antagonistic conflict . . . is transferred from the level of military clashes to that of economic competition, comparison of political systems and ways of life, and ideological struggle.[15]

In 1967, Yuri Andropov, then head of the KGB, and later Secretary General of the CPSU, is quoted as having said:

> . . . peaceful coexistence is a form of class struggle. It implies a bitter and stubborn struggle on all fronts – economic, political, and ideological. . . . The State security are obligated in this struggle to accomplish their specific missions efficiently and faultlessly.[16]

Lenin, in fact, believed that peaceful coexistence in its literal sense was impossible. As early as 1920 he declared that, as long as capitalism and socialism (i.e. communism) exist, there would be *no* peace until one of them triumphed. Soviet foreign policy statements have traditionally included repeated affirmation of the virtues of peaceful coexistence and cooperation between states with different social systems as an instrument of persuading non-communist countries to lower their guard. There has, however, never been, in the foreign policy of the Soviet Union, any disposition to believe that the confrontation between communism and capitalism can ever give way to a state of affairs in which the two systems can live together permanently in peace, which is what the term 'peaceful coexistence' would appear to signify. Gromyko, the long-serving *éminence grise* of Soviet diplomacy, who is now the President of the CPSU, summed up the situation admirably:

> Peaceful coexistence creates the most favourable conditions for the mobilization of the masses in the struggle against Imperialism, for a durable peace on earth. . . . For these reasons peaceful coexistence is a specific form of the class struggle of socialism and capitalism in the world arena, without turning to military means, to weapons.[17]

More recently Gromyko has been quoted by *The Communist* (the main Communist Party magazine) as saying:

> Peaceful coexistence is a specific form of class struggle by socialism against capitalism. Such struggle is going on and will continue in the sphere of economics, politics and certainly ideology – because the world outlook and class aims of the two social systems are opposite to each other and irreconcilable.[18]

CHAPTER TWO

Disinformation and Active Measures

The principal characteristic of the foreign policy of the USSR has always been its flexibility. Basing themselves firmly on Leninist teaching, Russian leaders have used every instrument of power – military, economic, psychological or diplomatic – to achieve their foreign policy aims. They are prepared to use armed force where they think it to be appropriate, and when they believe that they can use it with negligible risk to themselves. In Berlin in 1953, in Hungary in 1956, in Czechoslovakia in 1968, and more recently in Afghanistan, the use of Soviet military power has been a decisive factor, as was the threatened use of such power in Poland in 1981.

In the central confrontation between the Soviet Union and the West, however, the military option has been, for all practical purposes, unavailable partly because of the existence of the North Atlantic Treaty Organization, which has identified the United States clearly with the territorial integrity of Western Europe; and partly because of the availability of nuclear weapons, which pose the threat of total devastation in the event of an attack by the Soviet Army in Europe. It is for this reason that such a large part of Soviet propaganda concentrates on attacking NATO and its nuclear strategy.

Recognizing that there is no political aim in Europe which could sensibly justify the risk of nuclear war, Russian leaders have resorted to one of the classic doctrines of the political philosophy upon which the Soviet system is constructed:

Marxism–Leninism stands for the use of all peaceful as well as non-peaceful forms of struggle against Capitalism.[19]

Their methods have included the skilful manipulation of the

Western press and electronic media, the use of front organizations and protest movements, and a programme of what is known in Russian as *active measures*, which includes the technique of *disinformation*.

The terms 'active measures' and 'disinformation' are, to some extent, interchangeable; both are direct translations from the Russian. *Dezinformatsia* was the word in general use until the 1950s, when *aktivnye meropriatia* came into use to describe the whole range of political warfare techniques used by the Soviet Union against the West. As one of these *active measures*, disinformation consists of a specific set of operations, denoting false, incomplete or misleading information that is passed, fed or confirmed to a targeted individual, group or country.

The Soviet Union's definition is to be found in the KGB's own training manual:

> Strategic disinformation assists in the execution of State tasks, and is directed at misleading the enemy concerning basic questions of state policy. . . .[20]

Soviet analysts in the West have argued at some length as to whether the principal target of disinformation is the decision-maker or the broad masses. As the Soviet defector Anatoly Golitsyn explained at a conference on disinformation in Paris at the end of 1984, varying and competing definitions of disinformation are themselves sources of ignorance and confusion. His own definition, based upon his experiences during a varied career in the KGB, including four years in the KGB's 'think tank', sums up the matter very clearly and will serve as well as any other:

> The essence of such operations is an active misrepresentation of the true communist principles, goals and strategies in order to accomplish them by influencing and inducing their western adversaries to contribute, albeit unwittingly, to the accomplishment of their objectives.[21]

Strategic disinformation is generally controlled and coordinated by the International Department of the Soviet Communist Party together with the 1st Chief Directorate of the KGB. Disinformation is a total effort, in which the full apparatus of party and state is involved. It has long been known that a favourite and effective method for disinformation is the use of foreigners to promote, consciously or unwittingly, Soviet objectives. These are sometimes known as 'agents of influence' and may be either foreigners recruited as Soviet agents or 'trusted contacts' who consciously collaborate without being formally recruited, or alternatively individuals who are unwittingly manipulated. The International Department controls foreign communist parties and is responsible for front organizations, 'peace movements' and the Academy of Sciences; the KGB 1st Chief Directorate handles covert propaganda, 'agents of influence' and manipulation of the foreign media. This has been confirmed by the defector Anatoly Golitsyn, who has also confirmed, in Paris, that Russian writers, scientists and diplomats play an active role in the disinformation effort.

The device of the 'front organization' is the most familiar technique for this purpose. There are ten of these major organizations which, while represented as popular, democratic and politically neutral, are, in fact, committed to the promotion of communist policies and, more specifically, of Soviet foreign policies. The most powerful is the World Peace Council which was founded in Paris in 1949. It was expelled from Paris in 1951 and subsequently from Vienna in 1957 for subversive activities and now has its base in Helsinki. It is directed by an Indian communist, Romesh Chandra, and is firmly under the control of the International Department.[22] Its propaganda line is frequently reflected in the activities of 'peace' groups such as the Campaign for Nuclear Disarmament.

Another active front organization is the World Federation of Trade Unions, based in Prague. Its principal subsidiary, the International Trade Union Committee for Peace and Disarmament, otherwise known as the Dublin Committee, is designed to mobilize all world trade unions for what is known in its action programme as 'peace and disarmament' – in other words, to support Soviet policies on these issues. Two other front organizations worth mentioning in this context are the Christian Peace Conference, also based in Prague; and the

33

Women's International Democratic Federation, based in East Berlin, which aims to coordinate women's action in support of those familiar objectives of Soviet foreign policy – '*peace* and disarmament'.[23]

Military action is the preferred option in Soviet foreign policy *only* when it can achieve its aims at low cost, minimum risk and with a very high chance of success – as in Hungary, Czechoslovakia and Afghanistan. The West has demonstrated, through a combination of the North Atlantic Treaty Organization and a defence strategy based on nuclear deterrence, that any military attack on the Western powers would have a very high cost, maximum risk and a very low possibility of success. Indeed, at its worst, the cost to the Soviet Union might be total devastation of the homeland.

For these reasons, other forms of action are preferred. As Lenin said in 1920:

> from the point of view of the danger of a collision between Capitalism and Bolshevism, it must be said that concessions are a continuation of the war, but in a different sphere. Every step of the enemy will have to be watched. Every means of administration, surveillance, influence and authority will be required. And this is war.[24]

In 1969 Brezhnev indicated how this war should be directed:

> It is impossible to win in the struggle against Imperialism and to achieve the consolidation of the unity of our movement and all anti-Imperialist forces without developing a most active offensive against bourgeois ideology.[25]

There is, then, nothing new in the concept of political warfare. Lenin regarded tactical flexibility as a cardinal rule of communist policy, and referred specifically to the importance of sowing dissension and distrust among the enemy.

> The communist must be prepared to make every sacrifice and, if necessary, even resort to all sorts of cunning, schemes and stratagems, to employ illegal methods, to evade and conceal the

truth. . . . The practical part of communist policy is to incite one enemy against another . . . my words were calculated to evoke hatred, aversion, contempt . . . not to correct an opponent's mistake but to destroy him.[26]

It is important at this stage to point out that there may well be differences between what the USSR perceives and what it *says* it perceives. If the USSR is to rationalize its own foreign policies and the massive expenditure required to support them, the United States has to be characterized as militaristic, imperialist and aggressive. That, therefore, is precisely how the United States is 'perceived' by the Soviet Union.

The Soviet Union seeks to limit the power and influence of the West by exploiting to the full all the instruments of its own power and influence. It maintains a massive global military presence, with powerful ground forces in Eastern Europe, especially in East Germany; naval forces, including the most powerful submarine fleet in the world, in all the oceans of the world, including the waters of the Atlantic and Pacific Oceans around the United States. It operates a protean espionage organization under the control of the KGB (the Commission for State Security) and the GRU (the military intelligence arm). Many of the USSR's intelligence agents are based in, or controlled from, the heavily manned embassies which the Soviet Union and its East European allies maintain in all important Western capitals.

The USSR mounts a persistent campaign to minimize American influence in the developing countries of the Third World. This is carried on through intensive diplomatic activity, the supply of arms and military equipment, and continuous anti-Western propaganda. The Soviet Union also sponsors, encourages and exploits international terrorism, which has developed into a system of low-cost, low-intensity warfare against the United States and its allies. This phenomenon is dealt with fully in Chapters 4 to 6. Many case histories and confessions by captured terrorists confirm the existence of KGB-run training programmes for terrorists, both in the USSR and in satellite states, as well as support given by proxy via states such as North Korea, South Yemen, Syria and Libya.[27]

Every element in this complex machinery of Soviet foreign policy has to be taken into account by democratic countries in the formulation of their external and security policies. It is, however, the size, shape and strategic doctrine of the armed forces of the USSR which principally dictate the assumptions upon which the defence policies of the West in general and the United Kingdom in particular have to be formulated.

CHAPTER THREE

The Military Dimension

Even allowing for various differences of assessment and interpretation, it is widely agreed that the Soviet Union spends a much higher proportion of its national resources, both gross and per head of the population, on its military establishment than any other major power, and that it has demonstrated on more than one occasion its readiness to use its military strength ruthlessly and effectively in pursuit of its political aims.

It is possible, of course, to argue that the massive military capability of the Soviet Union is not of itself evidence of hostile intent. Some analysts advance alternative explanations – historic Russian paranoia about the activities of the outside world; the predominant influence of the military establishment in the Soviet bureaucracy; or a determination to ensure that any future conflict shall not be fought on Russian soil.

It is always difficult to arrive at an exact assessment of the intentions of any government, however open may be its processes of decision-making, and however irresponsibly incontinent may be its press and the loyal opposition. In the case of an obsessively secretive totalitarian power, with no free press and no opposition, it is virtually impossible. In the business of threat analysis, however, intentions cannot be separated from capabilities. Indeed, it is often possible to make a valid assessment of the intentions of a potential enemy *only* from a close study of his military capabilities – the size, strength and shape of his armed forces, their equipment, training, strategic assumptions and tactical doctrines.

In this context it is possible to assert as a general proposition that Russian military strength is entirely disproportionate to any possible requirement for the territorial defence of the Soviet Union, especially in the light of the military capabilities of any potential aggressor. More specifically, any careful examination of the equipment, deployment, tactical doctrines and training methods of the Soviet armed forces seems clearly to suggest an aggressive posture. For example, while the annual manoeuvres of the NATO forces in Europe are regularly based upon a battle plan involving an early withdrawal in the face of a Soviet attack, followed by a defensive battle and counter-attack, Soviet and Warsaw Pact military exercises include no such defensive phase. They are designed to train military formations in rapid advance, assault, river crossings, airborne operations ahead of the main force and the use of chemical weapons to neutralize defensive positions. It may be, of course, that this can be explained by the determination of Russians to fight a defensive battle on the soil of her adversaries rather than on that of Mother Russia, but it would be unwise to draw too much comfort from such a theory.

Furthermore, the Soviet Union has consistently demonstrated its readiness to use its military capabilities aggressively in any situation in which it cannot clearly and effectively be deterred from doing so. It is sometimes argued that this expansionist tendency springs more from pragmatism and opportunism than from any strategic blueprint, and that it is part of a defensive mechanism designed to pre-empt and neutralize the activity of potential aggressors in the West and the Far East. Those who advance this argument apparently discount the evidence of a number of defectors and dissidents from the Soviet Union and Eastern Europe who have provided persuasive, if not entirely conclusive, evidence of the existence of a grand design for global predominance.

Whether or not this is so, it is important to recognize that a confrontation exists. We are engaged with the Soviet Union in a continuing conflict of faith, of ideas and of moral values; a conflict between two totally irreconcilable political systems, one in which the individual exists only to serve the state, and one in which the state exists to serve the individual. These two systems might conceivably coexist in something resembling uneasy stability, but there can never be compromise with the values of totalitarianism. It is entirely fanciful to suppose that in the next ten or fifteen years some miraculous transformation will occur, and that the confrontation between Soviet imperialism and the free world will cease to exist.

The conclusion of any prudent Western government must therefore be that the military strength of the Soviet Union, in the context of its known doctrines and policies, poses a real and growing threat to Western security. This is not necessarily the threat of a sudden assault by the Warsaw Pact forces in Europe, although such a possibility should never be discounted; it may not even be a threat of direct military action at all. The danger is of a more classical kind, deriving from the political significance of military power. If the Soviet Union is permitted to establish a decisive superiority in military forces, both nuclear and conventional, then the mere *threat* of military action, whether implicit or explicit, might be enough to ensure that it could achieve virtually unlimited political aims without the need to move a single division across a national frontier.

Some assessment of the strategic doctrines of the Soviet Union is therefore essential to the process of formulating our own defence policies. One of the principal deficiencies of a great deal of strategic analysis in the West is a persistent failure to appreciate that Russian and Western strategic doctrines are based upon entirely different assumptions, cultures and habits of mind. This truth was underlined by an authoritative Russian source in *The Penkovsky Papers*, published in 1965.

One thing must be clearly understood. If someone were to hand to an American general, and an English general, and a Soviet general the same set of objective facts and scientific data, with instructions that these facts and data must be accepted as impeccable, and an analysis made and conclusions drawn on the basis of them, it is possible that the American and the Englishman would reach similar conclusions – I don't know. But the Soviet general would arrive at conclusions which would be radically different from the other two. This is because, first of all, he begins from a completely different set of basic premises and preconceived ideas, namely, the Marxian concepts of the structure of society and the course of history. Second, the logical process in his mind is totally unlike that of his Western counterparts, because he uses Marxist dialectics, whereas they will use some form of deductive reasoning. Third, a different set of moral laws governs and restricts the behaviour of the Soviet. Fourth, the Soviet general's aims will be radically different from those of the American and the Englishman.

In a great deal of Western strategic analysis, many of the elements of any rational debate about nuclear deterrence, such as the disarming strike, ballistic missile defence, selective targeting, civil defence and the modernization of theatre nuclear weapons, are glibly dismissed on the basis that 'no one can win a nuclear war'. This statement is repeatedly uttered with profound conviction by distinguished scientists, retired generals and politicians of various persuasions. Yet it derives entirely from Western value judgements and habits of thought and plays a very minor part in Russian military thinking. A study of the most authoritative strategic writing from the Soviet Union – that of Sokolovsky, Ivanov, Gorshkov and Kulikov among others – indicates that the concept of fighting and winning a nuclear war has long been at the heart of Russian military doctrine. For the Soviet Union the only effective nuclear deterrent is one which confers upon those who possess it the option of fighting a successful nuclear war if deterrence should fail. Sokolovsky has written:

> We conclude that the Soviet Union's Armed Forces and those of the other socialist countries must be prepared above all to wage a war where both antagonists make use of nuclear weapons. Therefore, the key task of strategic leadership and theory is to determine the correct, completely scientific solution to all the theoretical and practical questions related to the preparation and conduct of just such a war.[28]

Brezhnev, like other Soviet leaders, frequently asserted that the USSR is a 'peace-loving' nation. The declared position which the Soviet

Union presents both to the West and to its own population is that the idea of a nuclear exchange is abhorrent and will result only in mutual destruction of East and West. A different attitude can be detected from a consideration of the work of military specialists whose writings are not intended for public consumption but are private statements of military policy.

From these writings it seems that, unlike the United States, the Soviet Union has traditionally believed that nuclear wars, far from being unthinkable, can be fought and won. From internal USSR sources it appears that this belief is inherent in Soviet foreign policy. For example, in 1972 the Soviet military writer General Milovidov, who was directing studies of Marxist–Leninist philosophy at the Lenin Military–Political Academy and who therefore undoubtedly spoke with the official sanction of the CPSU, wrote:

> There is profound error and harm in the disorienting claims of bourgeois ideologues that there will be no victor in a thermo-nuclear world war. The peoples of the world will put an end to Imperialism, which is causing mankind incalculable suffering.[29]

In 1973 another military authority, Colonel Skirdo, who was a senior instructor at the General Staff Academy of the Soviet Union and therefore also wrote with official sanction, underlined the point:

> Today's weapons make it possible to achieve strategic objectives very quickly. The very first nuclear attack on the enemy may inflict such immense casualties and produce such vast destruction that his economic, moral, political and military capabilities will collapse, making it impossible for him to continue the struggle, and presenting him with the fact of defeat.[30]

And in 1974 General Kulikov, who was a full member of the Central Committee of the CPSU and who therefore spoke with official approval, introduced into the concept of nuclear war-fighting the principles of political control:

> Today, bourgeois military theoreticians maintain that, with the

41

development of nuclear missiles, somehow it is not possible for policy to control and direct military strategy. Such claims are groundless. . . . Moreover, the appearance of modern means of destruction is increasing the determining role of policy in relation to strategy.[31]

This was reinforced a year later by Colonel Tyushkevich, writing in *Communist of the Armed Forces*, whose words can safely be taken to reflect the official position:

The correlation of war and politics is fully valid under conditions where weapons of mass destruction are applied. The enormous might of the means of destruction leads . . . also to the enhancement of the role of politics in the leadership of war, for now, immeasurably more effective means of struggle are at the disposal of the state power.[32]

More recently Marshal Ogarkov underlined these doctrines in the current edition of the *Soviet Military Encyclopedia* (1979). Although Ogarkov was removed from his position as Chief of the General Staff in 1984, his writing on military affairs continues to be published. In an article in the *Encyclopedia* on 'Military Strategy' he wrote:

It is taken into account that with modern means of destruction nuclear war might be comparatively short. However . . . it is not excluded that it might be protracted also. . . . The Soviet Union and fraternal states in this event will have, in comparison with imperialist states, definite advantages. . . . This creates for them objective possibilities for achieving victories.

In other words, nuclear war remains not only thinkable, but winnable.

While it would be wrong to ascribe to these writings the full weight of central strategic planning in the Soviet Union, original and iconoclastic thought is not encouraged in the Soviet armed forces, and it can reasonably be assumed that the writers (who were all serving officers in the armed forces at the time of their writing) were reflecting the received wisdom of the day. They could not have published these views unless they had official sanction.

One of the logical conclusions which may be drawn from this acceptance of the possibility of an organized, politically controlled nuclear war is that the Soviet Union might also contemplate a 'first strike', designed to destroy a substantial part of any retaliatory force before it could be used. This would, after all, be the obvious way to go about 'winning' a war with the use of nuclear weapons. Much of the development of the Soviet offensive nuclear forces has lent weight to this conclusion. For example, the Soviet Union has placed emphasis on land-based intercontinental ballistic missiles of great penetration and accuracy especially suitable for attacking American missile sites rather than for retaliating against cities in the United States. It has to be concluded, therefore, that the Soviet Union has probably never subscribed to the concept of mutual deterrence, and it may now have something approaching the capacity to launch a first strike against the United States and, by extension, of course, against the United Kingdom.

It would therefore be foolish to base any defence planning on the assumption that the Soviet Union will not be the first to use nuclear weapons, however insistent their public statements to this effect might be.

The Soviet Union, faithful to its Marxist–Leninist principles, will employ *any* instrument – political, economic or military – in pursuit of its foreign policy aims. If it chooses the military option, it will use *any* weapon – conventional, chemical or nuclear – which it believes will enable it to prevail.

CHAPTER FOUR

◆

State-Sponsored Terrorism

One of the characteristics of a substantial body of radical opinion in the West is a reluctance to entertain the proposition that Marxism-Leninism is still the power which motivates the foreign policies of the Soviet Union. Sooner than admit this, apologists advance the proposition that the Soviet Union is a pragmatic power, uninhibited by the constraints of ideology. This leads to such notable eccentricities as the theory that Soviet military policies are essentially defensive in nature, inspired by legitimate concerns such as fear of encirclement and a determination to avoid any repetition of the dreadful experiences of the Second World War. In order to believe this, it is necessary either to ignore or to discount a massive corpus of Russian political and strategic literature; it is necessary, in fact, to make the somewhat dubious assumption that Soviet leaders mean what they say only when they are being disarming and ingratiating.

By a similar exercise of self-deception, it is possible to arrive at some comforting conclusions about the attitudes of the Soviet Union to the role of terrorism in political activity. Some commentators insist, on the basis of some rather selective quotation, that Lenin was opposed to the use of terror as an instrument of policy. This fallacy is based upon his frequently expressed disapproval of individual and random acts of political violence, and there is no evidence to suggest that he was, in fact, any less convinced than Marx of the value of terrorism to the revolutionary. It is therefore not entirely surprising that the Soviet Union should be closely involved in the contemporary phenomenon of international terrorism.

There is nothing new, of course, in the phenomenon of political violence. As long as there has been social organization, force has been recognized as a powerful sanction in relations between tribes, religious sects, political groups and, more recently, nation states. Nor is there anything new in the use of force as an instrument of terror. It was not invented by the architects of the Russian revolution. It has long been the ultimate weapon of secret societies, criminal organizations, revolutionary groups and tyrannical governments. What *is* new, and profoundly disturbing, is the fact that terrorism has become a decisive factor in the central ideological and political struggle taking place in the world today – that between totalitarianism and liberal democracy. It is a weapon which poses almost as great a threat to the free world as the vast apparatus of nuclear and conventional forces which have been occupying the minds of strategists for the last thirty years. Yet it is not easy to convince democratic societies of the reality and significance of the network of international terror.

Indeed, another interesting ingredient of political attitudes in the West is a reluctance to contemplate, even in the face of apparently incontrovertible evidence, the possibility that hostile forces might actually be engaged in a concerted assault upon the fabric of democratic society. For many years those who suggested that the Soviet Union posed a military threat to the security of the West were labelled as hawks, cold warriors, or covert agents of that mysterious institution, the military–industrial complex. Today few serious observers deny the threat of Soviet imperialism, although their numbers are growing under the influence of the 'Gorbachev factor'. Similarly, it was for some time impossible to speak or write of the dangers of subversion and left-wing extremism without being accused of fascism, union-bashing or McCarthyism. That meaningless slogan 'reds under the bed' was ritually intoned as though it contained some decisive argument against the growing body of evidence. Nowadays, it is a commonplace that trade unions, political parties, centres of education and media of communication in the West have been systematically penetrated by Marxists, Trotskyites, anarchists and extremists of assorted disciplines.

It is not surprising, therefore, that there should be a widespread unwillingness to recognize the growth of terrorism as a systematic threat to democratic institutions or to understand that it is now an international phenomenon, sponsored and often directed by the governments of countries hostile to Western political interests. It is still possible to be confronted with the proposition that the threat of terrorism is exaggerated – one of the arguments for this somewhat complacent view being that terrorism has not, so far, 'succeeded in destabilizing a single democratic country'. Furthermore, there are claims that terrorist groups are independent phenomena, motivated by religious, racial or political conflicts of a local or regional kind, without any structural international connections or significance. According to one school of thought, the only way to eradicate terrorism is to remove the grievances which drive people to violent protest. There is, of course, a sense in which this approach has a kind of bizarre logic. If, for example, the state of Israel were to be liquidated it is possible – although by no means certain – that terrorism in the Middle East would cease; but this is not a notably helpful analysis of the problem.

In approaching the manifestation of terrorism the first impulse is usually to attempt to define it. As a result discussions on the subject often devote more time to semantics than to practical assessments of the phenomenon and the measures which are necessary to deal with it. Conferences on terrorism frequently waste hours earnestly discussing such arcane concepts as tyrannicide, the doctrine of the just war, 'state violence' and the nicely judged distinction between a terrorist and a freedom fighter. Much of this is logic-chopping; and it was definitively exposed by the late US Senator Henry Jackson at a Jerusalem conference on terrorism in 1979:

> The idea that one person's terrorist is another's freedom fighter cannot be sanctioned. Freedom fighters or revolutionaries don't blow up buses containing non-combatants; terrorist murderers do. Freedom fighters don't assassinate innocent businessmen, or hijack and hold hostage innocent men, women and children; terrorist murderers do. It is a disgrace that democracies would allow the treasured word 'freedom' to be associated with the acts of terrorists.[33]

In other words, terrorism, like an elephant, may not be easy to define; it is, however, not difficult to recognize. For those who, like Dr Johnson, will engage in rational discourse only on meticulously defined terms, the 1979 Jerusalem Conference proposed a formula which, although not universally accepted, is now widely recognized as a serviceable definition:

> Terrorism is the deliberate and systematic murder, maiming and menacing of the innocent to inspire fear in order to gain political ends.[34]

This may not entirely satisfy either the linguistic philosopher or the stylistic purist, but it provides an adequate point of departure from which to examine the problem.

Terrorism, by this or any similar definition, has intensified substantially in the last twenty years. Since the late 1960s, over a hundred embassies or consulates have been attacked or occupied; hundreds of government officials have been murdered, tortured or kidnapped; the President of Egypt, a former Chief of the British Defence Staff and a former Prime Minister of Italy have been assassinated; attempts have been made to kill the Pope and the commander of the US Army in Europe; embassies, government buildings, hotels, department stores and airport lounges have been destroyed by bombs; hostages have been brutally seized all over the world; and a British police officer has been murdered by a terrorist firing from the windows of the Libyan Embassy in the heart of London. Furthermore, as the attacks in Lebanon on the United States Embassy, Marine Corps headquarters and more recently in the Shi'ite area of West Beirut have demonstrated, the sheer destructive power of individual terrorist attacks has increased dramatically.

The geographical distribution of terrorist incidents is even more significant. Terrorism has indisputably become an instrument of low-cost, low-intensity warfare conducted principally against the West; and, as the US Secretary of State George Shultz said in an address to the Second Jonathan Institute Conference on International Terrorism, held in Washington in June 1984, 'If freedom and democracy are the

47

targets of terrorism, it is clear that totalitarianism is its ally.' There exists, incontrovertibly, a network of international terror. Its sponsors, its paymasters, its suppliers of arms, training and equipment are states which have a clear interest in destabilizing and demoralizing the West. This is not, of course, to suggest that every terrorist act which takes place in the world is centrally planned and organized. On the other hand, it is clear that there are a number of states which are prepared to exploit, encourage and finance political terrorism wherever and whenever it will further their aims.

Most important among these sponsoring states is the Soviet Union, which, through the agency of client states, provides substantial training facilities and generous finance. Until the Israeli Army invaded Lebanon in 1982 and effectively, if only temporarily, destroyed the power of Yasser Arafat, the military arm of the PLO had been receiving training at more than fifty courses a year in the communist world, forty of them in the Soviet Union itself. Documentary evidence supporting this and other aspects of Soviet–PLO involvement in international terrorism is contained in a study published in 1984[35] which reproduces many documents captured by the Israelis in Lebanon. The wider ramifications of the Soviet relationship with international terrorism have been carefully documented in *The Soviet Union and Terrorism*, an academic thesis by Roberta Goren, edited after the death of the author by Jillian Becker and published in 1984. The most comprehensive and detailed account of Soviet involvement, however, appears in Claire Sterling's definitive work *The Terror Network*,[36] the product of years of meticulous research. Here, the origins of the modern terrorist network are traced back to the Tricontinental Congress held in Havana in January 1966, where it was decided to devise 'a global strategy to counter the global strategy of American imperialism'. This was to be done through close collaboration with the Soviet Union, and the first observable result was the establishment in Cuba later in 1966 of a group of training camps under the overall supervision of a KGB colonel. Although Fidel Castro had been operating his own guerrilla training camps since 1961, this was the first evidence of direct Russian involvement.

Meanwhile, the Palestinians were setting up their own camps all over the Middle East and in Southern Africa; and the two developments coalesced in South Yemen, a satellite state under the direct control of the Soviet Union. To a complex of training camps established around Aden, came aspiring terrorists from the Baader–Meinhof group in Germany, the Red Brigades of Italy, the Irish Republican Army, the Basque ETA, the Japanese Red Army, and the Tupamaros from Uruguay.

It was not until after the Egypt–Israel conflict of 1973, however, that the Soviet Union began to assume a significant and direct role in the organization of the network, providing training for the PLO in the Soviet Union, East Germany, Czechoslovakia, Hungary and Bulgaria, and arming the entire Palestinian guerrilla force with Russian weapons. On the pretext of supporting a 'national liberation movement' the Soviet Union had thus begun the process of disseminating terrorist weapons and techniques, through the PLO, to the terrorists of Western Europe and Latin America. The network was further extended and strengthened by the arrival in the Middle East of large numbers of Cuban instructors. The process has continued and developed, as Claire Sterling demonstrates in a series of detailed case histories. Since the disruption of the PLO's military organization by the Israeli invasion of 1982, the centre of this worldwide operation has moved from Beirut, and there is substantial evidence to suggest that part of it is now based in Athens, where the Greek police have already identified members of ten Arab terrorist groups, including three from the PLO.

The emergence of an international terrorist network has had a special significance for Britain in the context of Northern Ireland. There is clear evidence that the IRA has had close links with the KGB as well as with terrorist groups all over the world, and still has an especially close and significant link with Libya, where equipment, arms and regular training programmes are provided. The clearest early evidence of this emerged in March 1973, when the Irish Navy arrested the Cypriot coastal vessel *Claudia* as she was attempting to land a cargo of weapons on the Irish coast. The cargo consisted of five tons of arms, including 250 Soviet-manufactured rifles. The owner of the *Claudia* testified that the arms came from Libya and were destined for the IRA.

There is evidence that one of the murderers of Lord Mountbatten, Thomas McMahon, was trained in Libya, and, indeed, the Libyan government itself has never sought to hide its Irish connection. After the IRA bomb attacks in London in 1976, the official Libyan news agency carried the following announcement:

> These bombs which are convulsing Britain and breaking its spirit are bombs of the Libyan people. We have sent bombs to the Irish revolutionaries so that Britain will pay the price of her past deeds.[37]

Although at the time Qaddafi sought to play down this unequivocal statement, he himself said in 1984, in a reference to the IRA: 'This is a just cause and we are not ashamed of supporting it with all the means we have.'[38]

The close IRA–Libyan links can be traced back to the early 1970s when Qaddafi's confrontations with Britain over the nationalization of British Petroleum led him to announce, at the celebrations to mark the evacuation by the United States of Wheelus airbase, that arms and support for the IRA would be available from Libya. These links have persisted, with variations of enthusiasm, until the present day. After the murder of the British woman police constable in April 1984, a Libyan broadcast contained the announcement that:

> The people's committees will form an alliance with the secret IRA in view of the fact that it champions the cause of . . . liberating the Irish nation from the tyranny of British colonialism.[39]

In the light of all this, and of the fact that IRA leaders have attended conferences of international terrorists all over the world (for example, in Florence in 1971 and Lebanon in 1972), it is perhaps a little surprising that the IRA is still regarded by some incurable romantics, notably in the United States of America, as a nationalist 'freedom' movement. Those who believe that there is some magical 'political solution' to the problems of Irish terrorism have evidently failed to understand the real political aims and affiliations of the IRA. As long as they continue to be supplied with arms, training and a safe sanctuary by the international terror network, and with money by well-meaning 'friends' in the West, they will continue to conduct their campaign of violence, unimpressed by any irrelevant 'concessions' which do not lead to the establishment of a Marxist republic in the whole of Ireland.

CHAPTER FIVE

———◆———

The Changing Face of Terror

The Libya–IRA connection is only one example of the constantly increasing involvement of governments in the network of international terrorism. At least three other governments in the Middle East – Iran, Iraq and Syria – have been repeatedly accused of sponsoring terrorism in one form or another. Apart from the obvious financial advantages to terrorist groups, the effect of this sponsorship is that they can count upon training, logistical support, intelligence and safe sanctuary on a scale which they could never hope to achieve on their own. Furthermore, they can now employ weapons of advanced technology and destructive power far beyond the limits of their own resources. It is firmly believed in American intelligence circles that the bomb which caused the almost total destruction of the American Embassy in Beirut originated in Syria.

This situation is exacerbated by progressive improvements in the technology of destruction. As long ago as 1976, the United States National Advisory Committee Task Force on Disorder and Terrorism[40] examined the possibility that terrorists might begin to make use of weapons of mass destruction. At the time the conclusion was that the probability of any group successfully combining the material resources with the requisite skills and motivation necessary to employ high technology in an act of terrorism was extremely low. Nevertheless the report of the task force recognized that if weapons of mass destruction ever *were* used by terrorists 'the results could strain the very fabric of society'. What they did not foresee was that, less than ten years after the publication of their report, terrorists would be able to count on the sponsorship of countries some of whose leaders are known to have been seeking to manufacture or acquire nuclear weapons.

Nor is it only the possibility of *nuclear* terrorism that now poses a threat to the fabric of society. Chemical and biological weapons are not as difficult to manufacture as nuclear weapons, and there have already been several cases in the United States of extremist groups being detected experimenting with chemical agents. When the Symbionese Liberation Army – the American terrorist group which abducted Miss Patricia Hearst – was finally tracked down by United States security forces, the equipment found at its headquarters included a library of handbooks on chemical warfare and detailed instructions on the construction and use of chemical agents. One of the factors believed in the past to have inhibited terrorists from using weapons of mass destruction is the volatile and unpredictable nature of nuclear, chemical and biological weapons. The terrorist has always placed self-preservation very high on his list of priorities. The delayed-action or remote-controlled bomb, the shot in the back and the soft target of a department store or a schoolchildren's bus have, generally speaking, characterized the activities of the archetypal terrorist.

The picture has been radically changed, however, by the emergence of the suicidal terrorist. From the Iranian revolution and the minority Islamic sect which engineered it came the Shi'ite fanatic, a kamikaze-type killer for whom death in the prosecution of the Jehad, or Holy War, is a passport to eternal glory. These were the perpetrators of the attacks in the Lebanon on the American marine base and embassy. In pursuit of the extreme aims of Islamic fundamentalism, they are prepared to repeat those attacks in any part of the world, with weapons provided by political and religious leaders for whom the export of the Islamic revolution is an article of faith. The development of this phenomenon entered a significant new phase in March 1982 at a meeting of Shi'ite religious leaders and revolutionary students in the former Hilton Hotel in Teheran.

Its principal aim was the launching of a holy crusade to cleanse the Muslim world of those nations which fall below the purest standards of the Islamic revolution. Iraq, already at war with Iran, was an obvious enemy; but Kuwait and Saudi Arabia, together with their Western friends, also figured prominently as targets for the Jehad. The nerve centre of this new terrorist network is the Taleghani Centre in Teheran which combines its ostensible role of a religious seminary with that of a transit camp for Shi'ite militants *en route* to training camps all over Iran, where they are indoctrinated in the skills of revolutionary warfare, including the use of lorry-bombs and other suicidal devices. They constitute a form of international terrorism which is, as yet, imperfectly understood by the nations which are threatened by it.

Apart from the fact that the Western mind has difficulty in comprehending the suicidal nature of Islamic terrorism, the Jehad presents a special problem in that it does not consist of a permanent or structured organization capable of being penetrated by traditional intelligence methods. Operations are carried out by *ad hoc* terrorist groups drawn for specific, one-time attacks from a variety of Shi'ite groups, such as the Islamic Amal Da'awa (The Call), Hezbollah, the Islamic Front for the Liberation of Bahrain, and the Islamic Front for the Liberation of Palestine.

Each individual cell, once it is formed, plans its own operations, financed and supplied with weapons and equipment from Iran. When an operation is completed, the group disperses, and only rarely do its members come together again for a subsequent attack. There is an elaborate system of 'cut-outs' and strict application of the 'need-to-know' principle – an essential ingredient of clandestine operations. This flexible cellular system has pressure points all over the Middle East and as far afield as London, Paris and Vienna. So far Western intelligence agencies have had little success in countering this type of terrorism which has been described as 'the most deadly force in the Middle East today'. The emergence of this mysterious phenomenon, a potent combination of religious fanaticism, fatalism and conspiratorial cunning, has provided a new challenge for democratic governments, already beset by international terrorism of a more familiar kind.

It is therefore not altogether surprising that the country which spawned this especially poisonous form of political violence should serve as a base for international revolutionary movements. One of the principal figures in the Taleghani Centre, Syed Mohammad Taghi Modarresi, is also prominent, together with leading Iranian ayatollahs, in providing training centres for foreign terrorist organizations, including the IRA, ASALA (the Armenian Secret Army for the Liberation of Armenia) and the Tamils of Sri Lanka. The universities at Evin, in the north-west suburbs of Teheran, and Shiraz are the major centres of theoretical training, with practical training camps in other parts of Iran. Modarresi has claimed, in an interview with a French magazine, that he can assemble five hundred suicidal 'faithful' in a week. He has also asserted that he is capable of blowing up the White House in Washington – a threat which no Western intelligence organization would be ready to dismiss out of hand.

There is little doubt that the emergence of Islamic fundamentalism as an element in international terror has corrected any tendency in the West to underestimate the threat. Yet it is a development which, in spite of the penetrating analyses of such authorities as Elie Kedourie, P. J. Vatikiotis and J. B. Kelly, is still the subject of much confusion in the West. As Professor Kelly said in a presentation to the Second Jonathan Institute Conference: 'There is a curious and deep-seated reluctance among Western observers or commentators to attribute to the governments and peoples of the region any of those characteristics which their history shows to be ingrained in their very beings.'[41]

Kedourie and Vatikiotis, at the same conference, advanced the proposition that terrorism in the Middle East is an institutionalized phenomenon, with deep historical roots, which it would be difficult to eradicate from the world of Islam.

Until the Jehad began to pose an international threat in the wake of the Iranian revolution, it had been possible to discern a measure of success in the operations of democratic countries against the terrorist threat. The concerted campaign against aircraft hijacking had substantially reduced the frequency of this form of terrorism (although the incident at Teheran in 1984, carried out by Shi'ites and almost certainly condoned, if not actually inspired, by the Iranian government, was an especially savage example of murderous ruthlessness). The Baader–Meinhof group had been effectively destroyed in West Germany and the Italian government appeared almost to have neutralized the Red Brigades. In Turkey, domestic terrorism had been brought under control, although attacks by ASALA on Turkish diplomats abroad still occur from time to time. Meanwhile the most significant event of all in the counter-terrorist context was undoubtedly the virtual destruction of the PLO infrastructure by the Israeli armed forces in their invasion of Lebanon in 1982. Although it would be entirely premature to suggest that the PLO has disappeared, its once predominant role in the network of international terrorism has been, temporarily at least, substantially diminished.

These successes have not, however, correspondingly reduced the general threat posed to liberal democracy by international terrorism. The combination of Islamic fundamentalism and state sponsorship has, on the contrary, led to a situation in which, as Secretary of State George Shultz has said, 'More of the world's people must today live in fear of sudden and unprovoked violence at the hands of terrorists ... the epidemic is spreading and the civilized world is still groping for remedies.'[42]

Furthermore, any belief that terrorism in Western Europe had been effectively dealt with has proved to be illusory. At least three terrorist groups – the Red Army Faction from Germany, the Combatant Communist Cells from Belgium and France's Action Directe are now believed to be collaborating in a new campaign directed principally against NATO. There is evidence, too, of links with Middle Eastern terrorist groups and also of involvement with the Italian Red Brigades. After the successful operation of the Italian government at least 300 *brigatisti* are known to have fled to France where they have found sanctuary in spite of repeated requests by the Italian authorities for their extradition. Some of the literature and operating methods of the new anti-NATO coalition bear a strong resemblance to those of the Brigati Rossi. A recent abortive terrorist operation in Athens was claimed by its perpetrators to be a demonstration of solidarity with the Red Army Faction, the Combatant Communist Cells and Action Directe.

Much of the failure of the civilized world to defend itself against this form of low-intensity warfare derives, of course, from the very fact that it *is* a civilized world. The crucial matter is the relative importance accorded to freedom and order in organized society. There is, for example, little doubt that if Irish terrorism were approached as a purely military problem the IRA could be smashed, probably in a matter of weeks; but life is not as simple as that. In liberal democracies, individual freedom is at the heart of the social and political structure, and the imperatives of order are often ignored or modified in the anxiety to ensure that the rights of the individual are not attacked or eroded.

Yet it is not possible to ensure the survival of individual liberty without maintaining a high degree of civil order, without which the rule of brute force quickly prevails; for the weak there is then no freedom. It is, on the other hand, possible to ensure a very high degree of order provided that the demands of the individual are ignored or subordinated; for this reason totalitarian states are not vulnerable to the threat of terrorism, since their rulers are prepared to respond with counter-terror. The dilemma for the liberal democracies, therefore, is how to devise methods of defeating international terrorism without seriously eroding the individual rights of the majority of the people.

Sir Kenneth Newman, Commissioner of the London Metropolitan Police, analysed this problem in a lecture delivered in London in October 1983.[43] One of his important conclusions was that, although individual liberties are important, it is dangerous to become so obsessed by them that we overlook the importance of communal freedom and security. He added, however, a cautious qualification. 'Emergency powers for terrorist situations', he said, 'are not inconsistent with a free society if they are authorized by parliament, their use is monitored and they are suspended or rescinded when no longer necessary.' This view is essentially that of the law enforcement officer in a parliamentary democracy. It is moderate, civilized and restrained. The question which must now be asked is whether it is not a little *too* moderate, civilized and restrained; whether, in fact, it can provide the intellectual and political framework for an effective defence against international terrorism. In his address to the Jonathan Conference in Washington, Secretary of State George Shultz appeared to express grave doubts. His proposition was that purely passive measures to combat terrorism were no longer adequate. 'It is time', he said, 'to think long, hard and seriously about more active means of defence . . . about defence through appropriate preventive or pre-emptive actions against terrorist groups before they strike.'[44] This attitude was clearly reflected in the Republican platform on which President Reagan fought his successful campaign in the 1984 Presidential election. It has also been expressed even more forcefully by Paul Johnson, one of the leading British authorities on the political implications of international terrorism, in an article in *The Times* of 10 August 1984, entitled 'Wanted: World War on Terror'.

Yet it will clearly not be easy for Western governments to adopt the draconian policies implicit in these attitudes. In the summer of 1984 the Subcommittee on Security and Terrorism of the United States Senate Judiciary Committee held hearings on a package of anti-terrorist measures proposed by President Reagan. The proposed measures themselves seemed modest enough. They included an Aircraft Sabotage Act, designed to implement fully the Montreal Convention already ratified by the United States government in 1972. A major obligation of this Convention is that parties to it assume criminal jurisdiction over persons who, having destroyed a civil aircraft, are found within their territories. The second measure in the package was an Act for the Prevention and Punishment of the Crime of Hostage-Taking, designed to implement the United States Convention of 1979. The third was an Act for Rewards for Information Concerning Terrorist Acts, framed to enable the US Attorney-General and Secretary of State to offer substantial monetary rewards for information about terrorist groups. The fourth and most important piece of legislation concerned the Prohibition against the Training or Support of Terrorist Organizations, a bill designed to prevent American nationals from providing 'services' (e.g. support, training, logistical assistance) to any terrorist group acting against the interests of the United States.

These tentative steps towards enacting legislation which would give the United States government the power to embark on a programme to defend itself, however passively, against international terrorism ran into immediate trouble. The American Civil Liberties Union argued against the bill prohibiting training or support for terrorist organizations on the grounds that it would erode the protection afforded by the First Amendment by granting to the Secretary of State 'the power to stifle dissent from the reigning foreign policy of the moment'.[45] Perhaps more significantly, in the context of the proposals for international cooperation, the Civil Liberties Union objected that one of the proposed measures 'would permit the use of the United States military services and intelligence agencies to conduct investigations in the United States with respect to hostage-taking that occurred in foreign countries and involved wholly foreign participants and victims.'[46] The later reaction of the editorial writer of the *New York Times* to the proposed legislation was to describe it as 'Last year's bad idea . . . to invade the liberties of Americans in the hope of finding a few who were secretly assisting terrorists'.[47]

Faced with this kind of Pavlovian 'liberal' reaction to a modest anti-terrorist legislative programme, the United States government cannot have great hope of implementing some of the more positive counter-actions reflected in Mr Shultz's views. When there was a suggestion that the United States should retaliate against the truck-bombers of the Lebanon by bombing their bases, the outcry was immediate. The most reasoned objection came from Mr Robert Kupperman, an acknowledged authority on international terrorism, who, in his testimony to a Congressional subcommittee in June 1984, agreed that 'the days in which terrorism was confined to isolated instances of disruption are over; increasingly it has become a form of low-intensity warfare against the West conducted by trained professionals rather than nihilistic amateurs, and, in some instances, orchestrated by states rather than radical sub-national groups.'[48] He went on, however, to argue strongly against any suggestion of military retaliation, claiming that the potential for escalation might confront the United States with a choice between public humiliation and outright war against the sponsoring state, which might in turn lead to the involvement of the Soviet Union.

CHAPTER SIX

◆

Meeting the Terrorist Threat

The phenomenon of state-sponsored terrorism has introduced a new dimension into a problem for which there is no easy solution – no 'quick-fix'. It is essential, therefore, to examine carefully the practical possibilities which exist for an effective response to the threat of international terrorism. The basic premise must be that, as the threat is clearly international, the only effective response will be one which is also international. No single nation is capable alone of dealing with a network for which national boundaries are relevant only when they provide sanctuary for the terrorist. Indeed, in democratic societies a certain level of violence may have to be accepted.

Terrorism flourishes most when it is employed against societies with strong traditions of individual liberty, societies which may have to countenance a limited degree of disorder as part of the price of their freedom. Over-reaction to minor terrorist threats may undermine that freedom, and do the work of the terrorist for him. The first requirement is to identify precisely the threat against which democratic society has to defend itself. This is not to engage in the pointless attempt to *define* terrorism, but simply to categorize it, and to decide what constitutes a real threat to security. The hijacking of an American aircraft by a frustrated or unbalanced Cuban refugee does not present the same level of threat to the fabric of society as the hijacking of an airliner to Teheran and the subsequent murder of two American passengers by vicious Shi'ite extremists. The murder of a policeman in Northern Ireland, however outrageous, is not the same as an attempt to murder the British Prime Minister and most of the Cabinet with a delayed-action bomb in a conference hotel.

To the extent that they can be prevented at all, isolated incidents perpetrated by maverick individuals are the concern of national security forces. To deal with major incidents, especially those which are clearly state-sponsored, international action is essential. Yet there exists, at present, no formal international body designed to deal with the terrorist threat. The United Nations, as Paul Johnson has declared with characteristic candour, is useless. Many of its member countries are themselves supporters and sponsors of terrorism. There may, on the other hand, be some validity in the various proposals which have been advanced for establishing an International Counter-terrorist Organization of some kind, responsible for coordinating the collection and exchange of intelligence on terrorist techniques, personalities and movements; and for mounting effective operations against terrorist groups.

Although on the surface an attractive proposition, this idea is fraught with difficulties. The first requirement in fighting terrorism, as in any other military operation, is high-grade intelligence. Yet it is in this field that international cooperation presents the greatest difficulties. A nation's intelligence organization is one of its most sensitive and vulnerable institutions. The array of intelligence sources, methods and techniques is jealously guarded, and full cooperation between countries is rare. Some countries – the United States and the United Kingdom, for example – share intelligence comparatively freely; there are, however, other countries, even within the Western Alliance, with whom neither would think of collaborating in the collection or collation of intelligence. Furthermore, intelligence co-operation is a delicate flower – it can be withered by one spectacular failure of security. Information about the movement of terrorist groups is already exchanged amongst some Western countries, and it is probably unrealistic to suggest that this exchange should be formalized in some kind of permanent transnational operation.

The arguments against the establishment of supranational anti-terrorist organizations do not, however, weaken the case for international cooperation. If the package of legislation presented to Congress by the United States administration were to be accepted and enacted, and if a wide range of democratic countries were to enact similar legislation, intelligence operations against international terrorism would be substantially improved. The proposal to offer lavish rewards for information about terrorists is no more than an extension of the common practice of paying for information which leads to the prevention of a crime or the arrest of its perpetrators. The proposal that all explosives should be required by law to contain 'taggants' (ingredients which would permit experts to identify precisely the source of an explosive even after it had been detonated) would greatly facilitate the task of national security forces investigating bomb incidents. The Montreal Convention, if more widely implemented, would reduce aircraft-hijacking dramatically.

A further fruitful area of international cooperation might well be found in the principles and practices governing diplomatic relations. The murder of the woman police officer in London in April 1984 had the immediate effect of concentrating the minds of political leaders on the anomalies of a situation in which the gunman who had fired the shots was able to leave Britain freely under diplomatic immunity, and to carry the murder weapon with him in the diplomatic bag. As a result, a Conference of European Ministers of Justice approved the *ad hoc* establishment of a ministerial committee to consider ways of improving the exchange of information on terrorism, and to make recommendations concerning the abuse of diplomatic privileges. At a subsequent Economic Summit Conference in London the Heads of State and Governments issued a statement declaring that they viewed 'with serious concern, the increasing involvement of States and Governments in acts of terrorism, including the abuse of diplomatic immunity'.

The two international conventions which now enshrine the historically acknowledged immunity of diplomatic envoys are the Vienna Convention on Diplomatic Relations 1961 and the Vienna Convention on Consular Relations 1963. They confer immunities on persons, premises, communications and possessions of diplomatic representatives and consular staff. In the wake of the murder of the woman police officer (and the bizarre incident which followed it in July 1984 when the drugged body of a Nigerian ex-minister was discovered at Stansted

Airport in a crate for which the Nigerian Embassy in London had claimed immunity) various suggestions have been made for radical changes in the Conventions, in order to shift the balance of their provisions and to reduce the immunities of diplomatic staff who are in breach of these obligations.

Frank Brenchley, a distinguished British ex-diplomatist, has examined the various proposals in a study carried out for the London-based Institute for the Study of Conflict.[49] He concludes that it would be unwise to attempt any substantial change to the Conventions, arguing that 'living with the consequences of a weakened Convention could be extremely unpleasant, even dangerous for the missions of law-abiding states'. He points, however, to a number of areas in which far more use might be made of *existing* rights under the Conventions. The size of suspect missions should be limited. The missions of suspect states should be required to give sufficient details of proposed diplomatic appointments to enable potential terrorists to be identified in advance and declared *personae non grata*. He also makes the obvious point that if, in spite of sanctions against individuals, a mission is still believed to be planning or engaging in terrorism, diplomatic relations should be broken off at once. The simple application of this principle would have emptied the 'Libyan People's Bureau' in London of its gang of assassins and saved the life of the woman police officer. It is clearly essential that measures of this kind should be agreed and coordinated among like-minded nations, in order to prevent terrorist states from transferring their gunmen from one capital to another. Similarly, it might be prudent to review the implications of the 1977 Protocols to the 1949 Geneva Convention, which have the effect of conferring upon members of certain 'national liberation movements' protection equivalent to that accorded to prisoners of war, even if such 'combatants' fail to comply with the conditions of wearing armlets or other visible signs, and carrying arms openly.

These and similar measures are, however, no more than a matter of revising certain international agreements or insisting upon their strict interpretation in order to shift the balance of advantage modestly from the terrorist to his intended victims. It is still a matter for serious consideration whether more active and violent measures should be used to prevent terrorists from carrying out their operations. As George Shultz has rightly said, 'Our morality must not paralyse us.' Most arguments against the use of pre-emptive or punitive action by democratic states rest on the assumption that such action must be overt and attributable and therefore a possible catalyst for further retribution and escalation. This is, however, by no means self-evident. The United States attack on Tripoli and Benghazi in April 1986, in spite of the apocalyptic warnings issued on all sides, provoked neither counter-attack nor defiance. Instead, it had the effect of persuading Libya, temporarily at any rate, that the price of international terrorism was too high. There are indeed powerful arguments for 'fighting terror with terror'.

International terrorists accept no law and no morality, and there seems to be no convincing argument against the use of clandestine and non-attributable operations to eliminate terrorist groups detected in the act of planning or preparing an attack, or to visit retribution on countries which sponsor such operations. As Paul Johnson has said, no terrorist should be able to feel safe anywhere, and no terrorist state should be immune from terrible revenge simply because it employs clandestine violence in place of the more traditional and familiar instruments of war.

An essential ingredient of this approach is that every like-minded democratic government should establish a high-level, ministerially directed task force, with a highly organized infrastructure of police, intelligence agencies and specialized counter-terrorist units of the SAS type. Some countries already have arrangements of this kind, but they vary in level, effectiveness and political weight. It is important that national groups should be in continuous contact with each other, and for this purpose there should obviously be some uniformity of method and organization.

The general conclusion must be that the liberal democracies of the West need to recognize the bleak truth – that war is being waged against them by international terrorist organizations, often manipulated by countries which have a direct interest in the destabilization and ultimate destruction of Western political systems. If they are to survive they must first recognize that a state of war exists and then prosecute it ruthlessly. Countries which are clearly involved in the sponsorship of international terrorism should be given a clear warning that they are placing at risk their commercial and economic relations with the West. Any political or economic sanctions which may flow from subsequent activities should be binding on the countries of the free world. The recent history of international relations demonstrates conclusively that sanctions imposed by one country alone are fore-doomed to failure.

It is perhaps not too extreme to add that unless the United Nations shows signs of becoming more effective and robust in its attitudes to international terrorism, Western nations will have to consider seriously whether their presence in the organization is any longer of value. It seems bizarre, to say the least, that the representatives of the United States, Britain and other members of the Western Alliance should be obliged to rub shoulders in New York with the delegates of countries which are known to sponsor and finance the murder of their citizens for political ends; or that their governments should continue to pay heavily for the privilege.

No commentary on international terrorism would be complete without some consideration of the role of the press and the other media of communications. It has been perceptively remarked that 'terrorism is theatre'. The terrorist needs a stage for his actions. His success depends upon public attention – which is one reason why he attacks innocent civilians. A soldier shot in the back in Belfast may merit a few lines in the national papers – probably none in the international press – and possibly a brief mention on the national evening television news programmes; but a restaurant or a supermarket bombed in a city centre, with women and children killed and mutilated, will get headline and prime-time treatment, together with full publicity for whichever group may 'claim responsibility'. The fact that this may cause revulsion and outrage among readers, listeners and television audiences is of no concern to the terrorist. The aim of terrorism, as Lenin said, is to terrorize, and the more brutal and apparently senseless the attack, the better it is for 'the cause'.

It might therefore be seriously argued that the media, and more especially the electronic media, should decline to provide lavish facilities for terrorist propaganda. The classic reply from the media apologists is that 'the public has a right to know' and that the duty of a journalist is to report the news. It is, however, possible to report events without providing the sensational and dramatic effects for which the terrorist is seeking. The instinctive reaction of the journalist is to give excessive and exaggerated coverage to any event involving violence and destruction. This has led to the accusation that there is a symbiosis between the journalist and the terrorist, whereas, as Sir Geoffrey Jackson has said, 'the true symbiosis for the news media is with freedom.'[50] This is not always evident, however, in television programmes, news broadcasts and leading articles. Indeed, Jillian Becker, a leading authority on terrorism, and author of *Hitler's Children*, has accused the British media, and specifically *The Times* and the BBC, of 'assisting the legitimization of terrorism'.[51] While this may be a somewhat extreme view, the credibility of the journalist is certainly eroded when the celebrated public 'right to know' leads him to provide a personal platform for the terrorist himself, on the basis that the terrorist, like the government or the police, has a right to state his case. This kind of insensitivity springs partly from a belief, shared by many practitioners of journalism, that there is some position of neutrality, or objectivity, as between the terrorist and the establishment which he is seeking to destroy; and that it is the duty of the journalist to occupy this position, dispensing judgement with magisterial authority.

The fact is that there is no such position of objectivity, any more than there is, to adapt a phrase of Winston Churchill's, any position of neutrality as between the arsonist and the fire brigade. Terrorism, like any other form of warfare, is a phenomenon in which the journalist in a free society must take sides. He must decide whether a news item, or even a scoop, is more important than defeating a menace to the fabric of that society. At a conference on Terrorism and the Media in the 1980s, George Watson, Vice-President of News, ABC, made a statement which seems to encapsulate the attitude of many journalists towards the problem of terrorism:

If we had understood and acted on our understanding of the grievances of the Palestinian people, it is possible that they might not have reverted to the acts of outrageous terrorism in which they have engaged. It is not, however, the responsibility of the media to decide that this lot is good or bad, and that we ought not to provide a platform for their grievances, even when they involve terrorist actions. Our basic responsibility is to report what is happening.[52]

It would be difficult to imagine a more vivid expression of mental and moral confusion. An opposing view was put much more succinctly at the same conference by Steve Rosenfeld of the *Washington Post*: 'If the purpose of terrorists is to send a message, we of the media should consider not sending it.'

It is at least arguable that in a free society, in which democratic processes exist for the redress of grievances, a free press should have no difficulty in establishing its moral position as between the society in which it exists and those who threaten to destroy that society by violence. The struggle against international terrorism is a total struggle; we have the right to expect that the Western press and media should be wholly engaged in it. The fact of being a journalist does not absolve a citizen from the need to 'decide that this lot is good or bad'. If there are those in the press and the electronic media who are prepared to contemplate with equanimity the possibility that violence might be justified as the only way of removing a grievance, real or imagined, they should also be prepared to contemplate the certainty that in a society ruled by brute force, theirs will be the first freedom to disappear. Unhappily it will not be the last.

PART TWO

The Global Context

CHAPTER SEVEN

Greece, Turkey and the Mediterranean

The East–West confrontation cannot be considered in isolation from the political and strategic context of the rest of the world. In formulating its overall foreign and defence policies, Britain has to consider the extent to which its security interests might be affected by regional problems both within and outside the immediate NATO area. These might involve the management of crises not directly involving the superpowers.

Although the term 'crisis management' is of relatively recent origin, crisis diplomacy often involving the deployment of armed force has always been an important element in international relations. Indeed, as Coral Bell, the Australian academic analyst, has pointed out in a perceptive essay,[53] the word 'management' might be considered somewhat misleading for the activity concerned. 'It carries too many overtones of calm, judicious consideration of the allocation of resources with a view to best long term advantage,' whereas, when a crisis actually emerges, this kind of approach is usually overtaken by a kind of semi-controlled panic, with decisions enmeshed in a shifting pattern of uncertainties.

The essence of a 'crisis' in international terms is that it is perceived to carry with it the threat of war. National crises may be of an economic, financial or social kind; and they may carry with them connotations of threatened violence. Crisis in international relations has been the subject of many attempts at definition. Alastair Buchan, formerly Director of the International Institute for Strategic Studies, defined it as 'a deliberate challenge and a deliberate response, of a kind which both sides hope will change the course of history in their favour. . .'.[54] Others have suggested that it is any situation which raises destabilizing forces in the international structure, but almost without exception crisis is defined as a development which threatens violence.

Coral Bell suggests that war-threatening crises may occur either in the central balance of power, or in regional balances of power, to which she adds as sub-categories 'intramural crises of alliances'. It must be emphasized, however, that these categories cannot be regarded as discrete or exclusive. Often, as in Suez in 1956 and the Middle East in 1973, a crisis in the local balance of power threatens to develop into a crisis in the central balance and to precipitate an intramural crisis in the Western Alliance as well. There are many strands in the fabric of any crisis, and management of that crisis will depend on how skilfully these strands are identified.

In approaching a problem of global crisis management, one of the principal aims is, of course, the avoidance of war – either regional or central. At the same time it is necessary to ensure not only that a war immediately resulting from the crisis is averted, but that the long-term possibilities of such an armed conflict have been reduced. The relative balance of power, especially when the adversaries are both members of an Alliance, has to be taken into consideration; and some attempt must be made to remove the underlying causes of conflict which provoked the crisis. One of the key concerns must clearly be to ensure that the ability of the Alliance to function effectively has not been damaged.

However, as Coral Bell points out, apparent successes in crisis management may actually have the result of perpetuating the conflict. This is especially so when the settlement of a local or regional crisis preserves the ability of the demonstrably weaker party to continue the confrontation. United Nations crisis management in Kashmir has almost certainly had this effect, and it may be a dangerous element in attempts at crisis management on the southern flank of NATO. Indeed, as Dr Henry Kissinger often observed, crisis management should arguably be less concerned with *avoiding* conflict than with nudging the conflict towards a resolution.

Within the NATO area there is one crisis point which threatens the interests of the Western Alliance even when the general confrontation with the Warsaw Pact is in a condition of relative stability.

The strategic significance of the Turkish Straits area can scarcely be exaggerated. The Black Sea Fleet is one of the four principal fleets of the Soviet Navy, and, in conjunction with the Caspian Sea Flotilla, it consists of an aircraft carrier, together with submarines, surface and air units as well as naval infantry (marines). The Mediterranean, at the same time, is one of the routine naval operating areas of the Red Fleet. The Montreux Convention, which theoretically controls naval traffic through the Dardanelles, has failed to prevent the passage of the Soviet aircraft carrier *Kiev*, which has evaded the terms of the Convention by being described as a 'helicopter ship' or an 'anti-submarine cruiser'.

The Soviet Union has thus succeeded for all practical purposes in securing access to the 'warm waters' which have been a traditional target of Russian foreign policy for centuries. In time of crisis or war, therefore, the Dardanelles would be a crucial 'choke point' for the containment of Soviet naval power. Turkey, since joining NATO in 1952, has been principally responsible for the security of both the Dardanelles and the Bosphorus. The security of the Turkish Straits, however, cannot be considered in isolation from the control of the Aegean Sea, through which Soviet naval units would also have to pass *en route* from the Black Sea to the Mediterranean; and it is in this context that the persistent hostility between Greece and Turkey assumes such great significance.

Although Greece and Turkey are nominally partners in the North Atlantic Treaty Organization, Mr Papandreou, the Greek Prime Minister, openly regards Turkey, and not the Soviet Union, as the principal enemy of Greece. The traditional antagonism of the two countries has been exacerbated in recent years by the proliferation of bilateral problems, including the conflict over the Continental Shelf and the mineral deposits in the Aegean Sea; the dispute over territorial waters; the question of NATO's command structure in the Aegean; the problems of the Turkish minority in western Thrace and the Greek minority in Istanbul; and, of course, Cyprus, which has brought Greece and Turkey to the brink of all-out war several times in the last twenty-five years.

In the 1980s three new developments have combined to increase the explosive potential of the Greek–Turkish confrontation. One concerns the air space around certain of the Greek islands. The Greeks claim an air sovereignty zone of ten miles; the Turks reject this, arguing that it should be only six miles. As Kenneth Mackenzie, a British expert on the region, has written, 'If a hot-headed Greek pilot should one day shoot down a Turkish jet in the disputed corridor, there is a risk of war by accident.'[55]

The Greek attitude to international terrorism has emerged as another major irritant in regional relationships. Athens seems, to some observers, to be replacing Beirut as a refuge and base for international terrorist organizations, and many Turks suspect that there has been encouragement in Greece for the Armenian terrorist groups which have assassinated some thirty Turkish diplomats or officials in the last ten years.

The ramifications of Armenian terrorism, however, have deeper implications than their effect on the relations between Greece and Turkey. There is mounting and convincing evidence of links between ASALA, the Palestine Liberation Organization and the KGB. As an instrument for the destabilization of Turkey and the separation of Turkey from the West, the Armenian cause is ready-made for Soviet exploitation. It has been suggested in Ankara that the Turkish government might react against what it regards as Greek encouragement of the Armenian terrorists by sending its own counter-terrorist squads clandestinely into Greece to deal with the problem. The possibilities of a consequent Greek–Turkish crisis are obvious.

Finally, new developments in the long-running Cyprus dispute have done nothing to ease the tensions. The declaration in 1983 of an independent Turkish Republic of Cyprus has complicated the relationships of Western powers with both Greece and Turkey. For the United Kingdom, one of the four signatories of the Treaty of Guarantee of 1960, the issue was especially sensitive, and the British government publicly deplored what they described as a 'declaration of secession'. Prime Minister Papandreou described it as 'a flagrant violation of all the agreements and UN resolutions'. The UN Security Council called for the withdrawal of the declaration, and the United Nations Secretary-General, Sr Perez de Cuellar, embarked on a series of discussions with the individual parties. These have, so far, had no substantial result and Cyprus remains one of the dangerous pressure points in Greek–Turkish relationships.

In spite of an historical tradition of philhellenism, there is a tendency in the United Kingdom, as in the United States, to take the view that Turkey is more important than Greece to the Western Alliance, principally because of the obvious geopolitical factors, but also because Turkey appears to be a more reliable ally. In spite of assiduous cultivation by the Soviet Union, which provides aid to Turkey on a scale far exceeding that to any other non-communist country, Turkey still regards the USSR (and not Greece) as its principal potential enemy. It has been prepared to grant to the United States important facilities such as a number of key military airfields and the system of five electronic surveillance stations manned by 3500 American servicemen, which help to monitor military activities in the Soviet Union.

Turkey, a predominantly Muslim country, has close links with many of the Islamic countries of the Middle East, and is therefore reluctant to allow its enlightened self-interest in the NATO context to draw the country into involvement in possible American operations in the region (such as the use of the Rapid Deployment Force) which are not directly related to the security of Turkey.

On the other hand, Greece, under Papandreou, has adopted an openly anti-NATO stance. While the formations of the Turkish Army which are not committed to internal security operations are deployed along the frontier with the Soviet Union, most of the Greek Army is deployed not on the frontier with Bulgaria, but in Thrace and the Greek islands to guard against a possible attack by Turkey. A Warsaw Pact descent through the Balkan States, in conjunction with a naval eruption from the Black Sea, evidently plays little part in Greek military contingency plans. Furthermore, Greece has taken an openly pro-Soviet line on the East–West nuclear balance, causing exasperation in many Western capitals, with an attempt in 1982 to delay the deployment in Europe of American cruise and Pershing missiles.

None of this is altogether surprising, since withdrawal of Greece from NATO is part of the official policy of Mr Papandreou's Pan-Hellenic Socialist Party (PASOK), and although Mr Papandreou recognized the dangers to Greece of implementing this policy on his accession to power in 1981, Greece must realistically be regarded as no more than a nominal member of the North Atlantic Treaty Organization. The defence agreement signed between the United States and Greece in 1983 provided for the continuation of the four principal American bases in Greece until the end of 1988. Mr Papandreou claims that the United States is committed to dismantle its bases, beginning in January 1989. Meanwhile, as his part of the deal Mr Papandreou secured $500 million in military aid, compared with the $280 million originally proposed by President Reagan.

The possibility of crisis in the region is obviously considerable. The worst case would be the withdrawal of Greece from the Western Alliance. PASOK is committed to a policy of non-alignment. As Thanos Veremis, a contemporary Greek historian, has written, 'There is little doubt that Greece will attempt to assert her independence from foreign influence far more than she has done.'[56] This would clearly lay the Aegean and the Mediterranean more starkly open to Soviet expansion from the Balkan States. At the same time, if Greece were lost to NATO, reinforcement of Turkey and Italy in time of war would be seriously disrupted.

Even if Greece does not implement its policies of non-alignment, the Greek–Turkish relationship provides a number of potentially critical issues which are ideally suited for exploitation by the Soviet Union. The latent hostility between the two powers might be exacerbated at any time by an incident in Cyprus, in the Aegean Sea or in the air space above it. At the very least we must expect a prolongation of the state of affairs in which NATO's two southernmost allies are perpetually on the point of being at each other's throat. This clearly offers opportunities, both actual and potential, for Soviet exploitation.

So far as the British government is concerned, any reaction must inevitably be within the context of any collective action by the Alliance as a whole. Apart from the presence of a military contingent in the

Sovereign Base Areas of Cyprus, Britain has no specifically national interest at stake in the region. In the event of any Soviet move in the area, Britain would, of course, play a part in the implementation of any NATO contingency plans. In the event of an armed conflict between Greece and Turkey, much would depend upon the *casus belli* and the actions of the two nations at the time.

Greece, with its total armed forces of 178,000 (including an army of less than 150,000), is unlikely to attack Turkey, whose armed forces, although notably ill-equipped, number over 600,000 (including an army of half a million men), even though, perversely, the Greeks might regard the Turks as their principal enemy. There is clearly no intention on the part of Turkey to invade Greece. On the other hand, it is impossible to discard entirely the scenario of the self-fulfilling prophecy, in which persistently hostile rhetoric from Athens, coupled with some provocative incident, might cause a future Turkish government to take precipitate action.

If such a conflict took place, NATO's principal role might be that of mediator, although it is not by any means certain that either country would be receptive to such attempts. The United States, in its attempts to placate the Greeks, has hinted that it would not 'stand idly by' in the unlikely contingency of a Turkish invasion of Greece; and, indeed, NATO's own responsibilities in this case are fairly clearly defined. Not only does Article 4 of the North Atlantic Treaty provide for Alliance consultation among the allies 'whenever, in the opinion of any of them, the territorial integrity, political independence or security of any of the parties is threatened'; Article 5 goes further in providing that in the event of an armed attack against one or more of them, the others 'will assist the party or parties so attacked by taking forthwith, individually and in concert with the other parties, such action as it deems necessary, including the use of armed force . . .'.[57]

Whatever action might be taken by NATO in these circumstances, it is extremely unlikely that any unilateral action could or would be taken by the United Kingdom (it is significant that when Turkish forces landed in Cyprus in 1974, Britain, although one of the four guarantor powers, with a small but well-equipped force on the island, took no military action). Indeed, it is arguable that military intervention by NATO in a Greek–Turkish conflict would bring advantage only to the Soviet Union. The most effective kind of crisis management in the region is likely to take the form of some kind of comprehensive resolution of the outstanding issues between the two countries. This would have to include greater Turkish flexibility on the territorial aspects of the Cyprus problem and greater Greek flexibility in the Aegean. It might also have to include the redeployment of the Turkish 4th Army which is seen by the Greeks to pose the main military threat; and the corresponding removal by the Greeks of patently offensive weapons from the islands.

This postulates, however, a political desire for a settlement which at present does not exist. It would require also the good offices of some outside body such as the United Nations or NATO; and in their present mood, it is unlikely that either the Greeks or the Turks would look kindly upon the idea of outside involvement in their affairs. The obvious conclusion is that, at least so long as PASOK remains in power in Greece, the Greeks will remain a somewhat volatile ally and a dubious asset to collective security; and the security of the southern flank of the Alliance will continue to be bedevilled by regional rivalries which the Soviet Union will assiduously exploit.

If the Warsaw Pact succeeded in dominating the Turkish Straits and expanding through the Balkan States to the Aegean Sea (and possibly the Adriatic as well), the integrity of the southern region of NATO, and with it the integrity of Europe, would be at risk. Vital lifelines of the West run through the Mediterranean Sea, bringing supplies of oil, minerals and food. The area lies astride the communications between Europe, Asia, Africa and the Middle East.

Until the end of the 1950s the Mediterranean was an area in which the West lived and moved with certainty and security. The combined naval power of Britain, France and the United States dominated the seas from Gibraltar to the Aegean, where Greece and Turkey stood unequivocal and firm. The sea lanes were further protected by British bases in Gibraltar, Malta and Alexandria, a French presence in Algeria and American installations such as an important air force base in

Libya. Britain still guarded the Suez approaches from Aden to Djibouti. Today, with the single and somewhat precarious exception of Gibraltar, all these land bases have been lost to the West, some to fall into unfriendly hands.

At the same time the Soviet threat and presence have grown. Although the Mediterranean has historically occupied a prominent place in the aspirations of Russian foreign policy, Soviet policy since the Second World War has included a systematic attempt by Soviet military power to operate freely there. The principal thrust of this activity has been to build a naval presence to challenge the principal Western naval presence which survives there – the US Sixth Fleet. As US Admiral William Crowe, formerly NATO Commander-in-Chief Southern Region, has pointed out,[58] the Soviet Mediterranean Squadron has grown in proportion to the rest of the USSR's naval power. In the 1950s the presence of the Red Fleet was insignificant. Today, on average, the Soviet Navy deploys between forty and fifty ships in the Mediterrenean, half of them combatant units, and eight to ten submarines.

The nucleus of this force is the Fifth Squadron, which basically consists of twelve to fourteen surface units (including two amphibious vessels) and eight to ten submarines, drawn mainly from the powerful Northern Fleet based at Severomorsk, near Murmansk; it is periodically reinforced, however, from other fleets, including the Black Sea Fleet. At its strongest it compares favourably with the American Sixth Fleet which consists of about forty surface vessels in aircraft carrier groups and one or two nuclear-powered submarines. The Soviet Mediterranean Squadron poses a real threat to NATO's ability to control the Mediterranean sea lanes and protect the land flanks of the regional allies. As Duygu Bazoglu Sezer, Professor of International Relations at Ankara, has written, 'The Soviet Fifth Eskadra has not only broken the American naval monopoly in the Mediterranean, but has triggered a debate among Western strategists about the future ability of the US Sixth Fleet to project power ashore and to keep open the sealanes....'[59]

Simultaneously with this military activity, the Soviet Union has pursued an active, although only partly successful, foreign policy offensive in the area. Both Syria and Libya may now reasonably be regarded as client states of the USSR; Libya is, indeed, one of the major forward bases for the storage of Soviet military equipment. Malta has, to a significant extent, aligned itself with the Soviet Union. On the other hand, Egypt and, less positively, Algeria, also targets of Soviet penetration, have remained outside the Soviet sphere of influence. The USSR has therefore not enjoyed unqualified success in its political offensive; the indications are, however, that it has no intention of modifying its policies. Admiral Gorshkov, the architect of Soviet naval power, has repeatedly emphasized the rights of the USSR as a Mediterranean power and the role of the Red Fleet in providing 'the foremost line of defence' of the Soviet Union against threats from the south-west.[60]

The implications of this for the Western Alliance are obvious. The Mediterranean carries half of the oil imported from the Middle East to Europe; it also carries more than half of the Soviet Union's imports and exports. Italy, Greece and Turkey have important economic links with the countries on the southern rim of the Mediterranean. The defence of the Mediterranean is therefore crucial to the integrity of the Alliance in the entire region extending from Italy to eastern Turkey. At present, it can be said that NATO enjoys a marginal military superiority in the area. In addition to the massive presence of the US Sixth Fleet, there are twice-yearly naval manoeuvres in the Mediterranean involving naval units from Italy, Greece, Turkey and Britain as well as from the United States. However, although the Warsaw Pact, and specifically the Soviet Union, is generally perceived as the principal challenge to the West in the Mediterranean, there are regional problems which cannot be ignored, and which might have an important bearing on the critical East–West confrontation.

The British military presence in Malta came to an end in March 1979. It was perhaps significant that one of the honoured guests at the ceremony to mark the departure of the British was the President of Libya, Colonel Qaddafi. Although the Prime Minister of Malta professed a policy of neutrality and non-alignment, Maltese relations with the Soviet Union and its client states underwent a significant change. While negotiating guarantees of neutrality with France and Italy, Malta concluded in 1981 an agreement with the Soviet Union providing for the development of 'relations of friendship and co-operation in the political, trade and economic fields'. Indeed, between the signature and ratification of the Neutrality Agreement with Italy in 1981, Malta concluded an agreement with the Soviet Union placing oil storage and refuelling facilities at the disposal of the Soviet merchant fleet.

These facilities were part of an extensive underground storage complex installed by NATO in the 1950s, and 50 per cent of their capacity was now placed at the disposal of the Soviet Union. When it was pointed out to the Maltese Prime Minister that, although Soviet *naval* units were not given direct access to these facilities, they could be refuelled outside Maltese territorial waters by Soviet merchant vessels using the same facilities, Mr Mintoff's somewhat disingenuous reaction was to comment that activities outside Maltese territorial waters were no concern of his government. Later, in 1984, after a period of somewhat uneven relationships between Malta and Libya, a treaty of economic and security cooperation was signed between the two countries. Malta undertook not to permit the presence of foreign military bases on its soil; Libya agreed to assist in the training of Maltese troops and to provide military assistance in the event of an attack on Malta. The clear conclusion must be that Malta has moved perceptibly into the sphere of influence of the Soviet Union and its clients; the indications are that that trend is likely to continue.

The dangers of a 'Cuba' in the Mediterranean therefore cannot be entirely ignored. If the Soviet Union were to gain a degree of political and military control over the island, even though Malta were to remain outwardly 'independent' and 'non-aligned', the balance of power in the Mediterranean would be substantially affected. Apart from the obvious threat to NATO's lines of communication in the area, the Soviet Union would have achieved a base for further subversive and destabilizing operations in North Africa, considerably assisted by the activities of Colonel Qaddafi in Libya. It is difficult to discern what steps, outside the normal foreign policy and diplomatic process, are open to the West to prevent this. Britain, despite its historical associations with Malta, could scarcely play a significant role. Maltese attitudes to Britain under Mr Mintoff were generally characterized by hostility and suspicion, and there are no signs that the state of affairs is likely to improve under his successor.

Gibraltar, by contrast, is a country in which Britain has clearly defined national interests and responsibilities. At the beginning of the eighteenth century Gibraltar was occupied by Britain during the War of the Spanish Succession and subsequently ceded under the Treaty of Utrecht in 1713. Ever since, the Rock has been a persistent irritant in Anglo-Spanish relations. The latest phase began in the 1960s, when, in response to a UN resolution, talks between the two countries about the future of Gibraltar began. In 1969, with the discussions getting nowhere, General Franco closed the frontier between Gibraltar and Spain. The Lisbon Agreement of 1980 paved the way for the resumption of negotiations in 1982. After a delay brought about by the Falklands war with Argentina, the border with Spain was reopened to pedestrians in December 1982 and finally fully reopened in February 1985.

Meanwhile the climate of Anglo-Spanish relations had been changed by the accession of Spain to NATO and the European Economic Community. In the course of the debate in Spain on the accession to NATO, the Spanish Prime Minister, Sr Calvo Sotelo, told the Cortes that Spain in NATO would have a better chance of solving the Gibraltar problem than it would have from a position of neutrality.[61] On 27 November 1984, as part of an agreement reached in the margin of a meeting held in Brussels to discuss terms of entry into the EEC for Spain and Portugal, Britain undertook to discuss with Spain the issue of sovereignty over Gibraltar; and in February 1985, coinciding with the reopening of the border, talks began between the British and the Spanish Foreign Ministers.

The Gibraltar situation therefore seems, for the moment, to be relatively stable. Gibraltar, unlike Malta, does not threaten to slide into the Soviet sphere of influence. The only danger, at present remote, is that two members of NATO might come into confrontation over the Rock. Spain has not relinquished its claim to restitution of the territory; while the British Prime Minister, Mrs Thatcher, has made clear that there can be no question of a change of sovereignty without the full consent of the people of Gibraltar. This carries overtones of the Falklands issue, to which the Gibraltar problem has often been compared; and the only foreseeable danger is that some future Spanish government might, in certain circumstances, attempt to occupy Gibraltar by force – a development to which Britain, at least under its present government, would react strongly. However, with Spain safely installed both in NATO and the EEC, the possibility of such a crisis is remote.

Furthermore, Gibraltar has lost some of the strategic importance which it enjoyed in the past. Indeed, in 1981 Britain had already decided to dispense with its dockyard facilities there, and although 'The Rock' remains a 'choke point' between the Mediterranean and the Atlantic, it probably now has little more significance than the rest of the Iberian peninsula. It seems unlikely, therefore, that Gibraltar will, in the foreseeable future, become a focus of crisis.

CHAPTER EIGHT

North Africa

The North African Arab States, collectively known as the Maghreb, are rich in crisis potential. They have been the centre of Soviet political activity since the 1960s, just as the Mediterranean to the north has been the scene of increasing naval activity. Egypt, Algeria and Libya have all been targets of Soviet penetration. Egypt and Algeria were drawn into the communist sphere of influence but subsequently moved out again in the 1970s, Egypt expelling its Soviet 'advisers' and becoming overtly pro-Western, while Algeria has opted for non-alignment. Libya, under the erratic Colonel Qaddafi, has become for all practical purposes a Soviet client state. Meanwhile Morocco has pursued mainly pro-Western policies and Tunisia, under President Bourguiba has remained relatively stable, resolving a long-standing border dispute with Algeria in a twenty-year treaty of friendship signed in 1983. The two main crisis points in the Maghreb are undoubtedly Libya and the western Sahara, the centre of a dispute which involves Morocco and, indirectly, Algeria.

The history of Libya's involvement with the Soviet Union over the last ten to fifteen years is well documented. Until the end of the 1960s the West had, to a great extent, succeeded in denying to the Soviet Union control over that sector of the Mediterranean coast between Tripoli and Tobruk which is necessary for the interdiction of free passage between the Atlantic and the east Mediterranean. In September 1969, however, the Soviet Union embarked upon an involvement with Libya which has become progressively closer and more dangerous to the West. Indeed Colonel Qaddafi, then in the process of seizing power in Libya, attributed Britain's failure to come to the rescue of King Idris to the presence of the Soviet Navy which was, coincidentally, conducting manoeuvres off the coast of Libya.

Soviet tanks and instructors appeared in Tripoli in 1970, and Libyan armed forces began a series of training courses in East Germany. It was in 1974, however, that the Soviet–Libya axis entered into a new phase with the visit to Moscow of the Libyan Premier, Major Abdul Salam Jallud. Until this time, relations between Libya and the USSR had been persistently soured by Colonel Qaddafi's violent attacks on communism. However, the communiqué following Jallud's visit referred to 'the identity or closeness of the positions of the Soviet Union and the Libyan Arab republic on the most important international problems'. Although the communiqué made no reference to Soviet military aid, Russian surface-to-air missile systems were installed in mid-1974 around the main base of the Libyan Air Force (the former US Wheelus Field).

By 1975 Libya had acquired Soviet training aircraft and two squadrons of fighter ground-attack aircraft, and a large amount of military and naval equipment. Since 1976, the Soviet Union has been constructing an extensive military infrastructure in Libya. A new air base became operational in 1979; naval docking facilities have been established for the Soviet Mediterranean Squadron. In effect, Libya has become an essential logistical base and staging post for future Soviet operations in the Mediterranean and in Africa. The vast quantity of Soviet and Warsaw Pact arms supplied to Libya far exceeds the requirements of Libyan security forces.

Meanwhile Colonel Qaddafi has acquired a deserved reputation as a sponsor of international terrorism, dissidence and subversion. Libya's military intervention in Chad in 1983 met with the full approval of the Soviet Union, and although Colonel Qaddafi was forced by the French to withdraw in September 1984, Libya's continuing claim to the Aozou Strip (a sixty-mile-wide stretch of mountainous desert on the northern border of Chad) might still prove to be a focus of contention.

The intervention in Chad is characteristic of Colonel Qaddafi's capacity for destabilization in Africa and the Middle East. As Brian Crozier, the British expert on Soviet active measures, has pointed out,[62] Libyan activities have included involvement in attempted coups in Egypt and the Sudan; financing of subversive groups in Egypt;

attempts on the lives of the Presidents of Egypt and the Sudan; supply of money and weapons to Palestinian groups in Lebanon; transfer of arms to the People's Democratic Republic of Yemen for use against Oman. Nor does Colonel Qaddafi restrict his activities to his own region. Weapons and equipment of Soviet origin have been sent from Libya to terrorist organizations in South-East Asia, Europe and East Africa. Libya has been, in fact, a training ground and safe haven for international terrorism; numerous terrorist outrages all over the world have eventually been traced, in one way or another, to Colonel Qaddafi.

Libya's potential for provoking crisis is almost unlimited. Whether it arises from the claims to the Aozou Strip, a military adventure against Egypt, a Libyan-sponsored terrorist outrage, or an incident at sea or in the air off the Libyan coast involving the US Sixth Fleet, Libya will seem constantly to be on the verge of some chaotic and catastrophic entanglement. So far Colonel Qaddafi's taste for dangerous living does not seem to have been much modified by Libya's conclusion of a treaty of federation with Morocco in August 1984, a link which caused concern in many Western countries, but which it was hoped might have a restraining influence on Qaddafi's erratic foreign policies. The treaty has since been abandoned as an unsuccessful experiment. The King of Morocco has a more statesmanlike world view than that of Colonel Qaddafi.

Morocco, the westernmost of the Maghreb states, and the only one with an Atlantic as well as a Mediterranean coastline, is of unmistakable political and strategic importance. Culturally, as well as geographically, it lies at the confluence of Europe and Africa; it also lies astride the Arab and African world. At its northernmost tip it is only a few miles from Spain, and at Tangier forms the southern part of the Gibraltar Straits choke point.

Under King Hassan II, Morocco has emerged as an absolute monarchy, but with a constitution which prohibits the establishment of a single-party system of the kind which exists in neighbouring Algeria as well as in many other African states. Although the King has sweeping powers, Morocco is a truly pluralist state which guarantees individual freedom of worship, the right to vote and to join trade unions or political parties. The Moroccan Constitution, which is virtually unique in Africa, provides Morocco with a natural affinity with the West.

The stability of the country is threatened by one principal political problem – that of the western Sahara. The issue lies principally between Morocco and an organization known as the Popular Front for the Liberation of Saguia el Hamra and Rio de Oro – the Polisario. The territory under dispute is an arid, but mineral-rich area on the Atlantic coast south of Morocco, which was, until 1976, a Spanish colony. When Spain withdrew, the territory partitioned between Morocco (the northern two-thirds) and Mauritania (the southern third). Immediately the Polisario declared an independent Sahrawi Arab Democratic Republic, which has been recognized by a number of countries, including a majority of the Organization of African Unity (OAU). What has happened since has been described by David Lynn Price, a British consultant on Middle East affairs, as 'virtually a proxy war between Morocco and Mauritania on the one hand and Algeria on the other'.[63] However, in July 1978 Mauritania renounced its claims to the area and Morocco declared the entire territory to be a Moroccan province.

Since 1979 there have been numerous clashes between Polisario and Moroccan forces. Morocco claims that the Polisario are no more than mercenaries in the pay of Algeria, which supports them politically and provides them with training and shelter. The issue has therefore become a focus of bilateral dispute, with Morocco refusing to negotiate directly with the Polisario, and Algeria refusing to negotiate with Morocco. Although Morocco has agreed to a referendum to legitimize its claim to the western Sahara, there is no immediate prospect of a compromise. The war is going badly for the Polisario, but it is also proving costly for Morocco, whose basic economic weakness is exacerbated by the constant drain on scarce resources. The probability is that intermittent guerrilla activity by the Polisario will continue; and that this will present a constant danger of friction and possible crisis between Morocco and Algeria. The interests of the West are clearly involved here. Socialist Algeria maintains certain links with the Soviet

Union, although it is by no means to be considered as residing within the Soviet sphere of influence. Morocco is, in strategic terms, a valuable asset to the West. As well as having to deal with the destabilizing potential of the western Sahara problem, Morocco, like many other countries in the region, is under threat from the more militant aspects of Islamic fundamentalism.

So far as Britain is concerned, there is little possibility of any independent or decisive role in the Mahgreb. Relations with the countries of the region are good except, of course, in the case of Libya, whose involvement in the murder of a police officer in London in 1984 brought about a rupture of diplomatic relations. Relations with Morocco are normal, although not as close as those of France, which is Morocco's principal trading partner, and probably has as much political influence in Rabat (and Algiers) as any other country, including the OAU and the Arab States.

CHAPTER NINE

Islam and the Middle East

The main crisis in the Middle East continues to be the confrontation between Israel and the Arab States, together with the Iran–Iraq war and its implications for the security of the Gulf and the unhindered supply of Middle East oil to Europe. These are, of course, potential flashpoints of great importance. Except in the most general sense, however, they do not have a significant impact on the formulation of British defence policy, since Britain is unlikely to become militarily involved in either confrontation unless it should erupt into general war as a result of the actions of one or both of the superpowers. This study therefore concentrates on another aspect of the Middle East: the role of Islam in two areas which might prove to be a catalyst for further instability – the rise of Sh'ite militancy, and the aspirations of the Kurds.

The rise, in the 1970s and 1980s, of Islamic fundamentalism is widely perceived as a systematic rejection of the Western values and philosophies which had been imported into many Islamic countries. Robert Olson, Associate Professor of Middle Eastern History at the University of Kentucky, sums up this view: '. . . the "re-politicalization" of Islam was, and is, primarily due to the combination of developments which enabled the Middle East to be dominated by pro-Western groups – Europe, Israel and the United States – during the 1970s.'[64]

In its simplest form the phenomenon represents a return to the *fundamental* values or precepts of Islam. It has, however, assumed a wide variety of outward forms, varying from the establishment of an Islamic Republic in Iran and the subsequent export from that country of Shi'ite militancy in the form of international terrorism, through the simple reimposition of Muslim law, often in its most draconian manifestations, to more liberal and moderate interpretations of God's will.

The two main groups adhering to the Islamic faith are the Sunnis and the Shi'a. The Sunnis, about 650 million strong, are often referred to as 'orthodox' Muslims, since they follow the practice of the Prophet as defined in the Hadith, or Traditions. They form the majority of the Muslim population in all countries except Iraq, Lebanon, Bahrain and Iran. The Shi'a, about 90 million strong, believe that the spiritual and temporal leadership of Islam is vested by divine command in Imams descended from Ali, the son-in-law of Mohammed (hence Shi' at Ali, the party of Ali). Of the Shi'a, the largest group (about 50–60 million) are the Imamis, or 'Twelvers', who believe that the twelfth Imam disappeared, but will one day return to inaugurate an ideal regime of perfect justice. Until that happens, all governments are rejected by the Imamis as illegitimate – although those which follow the advice of religious leaders are less objectionable.

These are the beliefs which helped to fuel the revolution against the Shah of Iran in 1979. Imami doctrine has been the state religion of Iran since the sixteenth century, but, under the influence of Ayatollah Khomeini's extremist and activist doctrines, it has become not only the mainstay of the present political structure of Iran, but also the source of the militant and often violent Islamic activism which is now beginning to destabilize the Middle East.

The Kurds, who number about ten million, represent significant proportions of the populations of Turkey, Iran and Iraq, with smaller numbers in Syria, the Soviet Union and Lebanon. They are concentrated mainly in eastern Turkey and the contiguous areas of the surrounding states. The majority of Kurds are Sunni Muslims, although some in Iran are Shi'a. They were left distributed around the Middle Eastern states by the creation of new national boundaries after the Second World War, and they have since been seeking a national identity. The principal Kurdish nationalist movements in Iraq, Iran and Turkey have, however, functioned largely independently of each other, although there has been considerable cross-border activity. They have posed a serious threat to central government only in Iraq.

The Kurds in Iraq have, in fact, been at odds with the government since the end of the Ottoman Empire. The Kurdistan Democratic

Party, formed after the 1958 revolution, has consistently aligned itself with opposition parties, including the Communist Party of Iraq. It is the largest and best equipped of the Kurdish groups, with an armed guerrilla wing of over 20,000 members at the height of its activities, and it has continued its struggle in spite of the setting up of a Kurdish Legislative Council in 1974.

The struggle entered a new phase with the outbreak of the war between Iran and Iraq. The Iranians, who had withdrawn support in 1975, now began to provide assistance once more, and in 1981 an alliance was formed between the various Kurdish groups, including the KDP, the militant Shi'a opposition group Al Da'wa and other Iraqi dissident organizations. As a result, the government, preoccupied with the Gulf War and reluctant to tie down forces in the north, has made significant concessions to Kurdish nationalism. It remains, however, a significant potential crisis point for the government in Baghdad.

The problem in Iran is even more acute for the regime of Ayatollah Khomeini. While Azerbaijan and Kurdistan were under Soviet control, a degree of nationalist independence was encouraged; the democratic republic of Azerbaijan was established, and the Kurds were allowed to set up the autonomous Republic of Mahabad. However, when the Soviet Union withdrew in 1946, the Iranian Army returned to the area. The President of Mahabad was hanged, the republic collapsed, and central government from Teheran was reimposed.

The Iranian Kurdish Democratic Party, ideologically inclined towards the Soviet Union, rejects the concept of a Greater Kurdistan, preferring an autonomous single Kurdish province in Iran; and when the Shah was deposed in 1979 the Kurds pressed their claims on the new Islamic Republic. After a few months of abortive discussions, Ayatollah Khomeini gave orders that the rebels should be crushed. The Kurdish forces have now been driven into the north-western mountains, their support lines from Iraq cut off. They present a continuing problem to the government, however, by tying up troops which would otherwise be used against Iraq.

In Turkey, which has the largest population of Kurds (about eight million), the government has never recognized them as a separate people or even as an ethnic minority, and has consistently discouraged any aspirations to separate identity. At the same time, although they display the characteristically turbulent temperament of their community, the Kurds of Turkey have never displayed any of the militant nationalism of their brothers in Iraq and Iran. Although they may represent a potentially destabilizing force, they pose no immediate threat to the Turkish government.

The Kurdish problem is regarded by the Soviet Union as a convenient instrument of destabilization in the region. It allows its own Kurdish minority a degree of separate cultural identity, in exchange for which Soviet Kurds have remained quiescent and isolated from other Kurds in the region. This permits the Soviet Union to give support in varying degrees to the Kurds of Iran and Iraq, while maintaining ostensibly good relations with the governments of Khomeini and Saddam Hussein.

The general conclusion must be that, although the Kurds cause minor irritation in Turkey and Iraq and somewhat greater inconvenience to the government of Iran, they do not collectively pose any immediate threat to regional stability. If, however, some dominant and magnetic figure were to emerge in their ranks and form the focus of a genuine 'national liberation movement' the situation might change radically. In such circumstances the Soviet Union would have increased opportunities for destabilization and expansionism.

A similar opportunity would be afforded to the Soviet Union by the emergence of a Baluchi National Liberation Movement. The Baluchis live in contiguous regions of Pakistan, Afghanistan and Iran. There are already reports of Baluchis being trained by Russians, Libyans and Yemenis. Obvious potential for destabilization exists in Iran (where the eventual disappearance of Khomeini might well lead to the emergence of a pro-Soviet regime) and in Pakistan, a nation so far West-orientated but beset by considerable economic and political problems. The Soviet Union, firmly installed in the Afghan part of Baluchistan, is ideally placed to take advantage of any changes in the orientation of Iran and Pakistan and to export Baluchi nationalism if it looks like bringing that about.

CHAPTER TEN

———◆———

Southern Africa

Southern Africa is one of the world's most important strategic areas. Apart from being the source of vital minerals, it dominates the Cape sea routes upon which the West, and especially Western Europe, depend for essential supplies of Middle East oil. In this area, the Republic of South Africa plays a decisive role. It has an army of 67,000, armed with 250 main battle tanks, together with armoured cars, armoured personnel-carriers and self-propelled artillery. It has the capacity, both technological and industrial, to produce a nuclear weapon and the means of delivering it accurately. Indeed, many well-informed observers believe that South Africa may already have carried out a successful nuclear test.

South Africa is faced with two threats to its stability – one from Marxist penetration into black Africa south of the Sahara; and one from internal unrest deriving partly from opposition to the policy of apartheid and partly from the activities of communist revolutionary groups. All these phenomena are interconnected. The revolutionary forces inside South Africa (principally the African National Congress) promote and exploit black resistance to apartheid; in turn they can expect help and support from many black African countries, especially the Soviet-orientated states of Angola and Mozambique to the north. There are varying degrees of instability in most black African states, whose tribal loyalties often conflict directly with their political boundaries, many of which are legacies of their colonial past. The major crisis point in the region at present, however, is in South Africa itself.

Internal developments in South Africa are of vital importance to the West. The South African government has a strongly anti-communist ideology; its geographical position, together with its basic economic strength and its rich mineral deposits, gives it a significance in Western strategic calculations out of all proportion to its size. If the South African economy should be seriously destabilized, or the present political structure radically undermined, the country, which is already a primary target of Soviet foreign policy, would quickly become vulnerable to communist penetration. The African National Congress, one of the principal vehicles of black political activism in South Africa, is largely communist-orientated and -inspired.

It is principally for these reasons that Western governments are concerned to press for political reform in South Africa. They recognize that the policy of separate development, or apartheid, might prove to be a catalyst for violent revolution and the creation of a situation conducive to the emergence of a black government with strong Soviet affiliations. The attitudes of Western governments are further affected by the activities of vociferous anti-apartheid pressure groups motivated partly by a genuine concern for human rights but also, in some cases, by a desire to see the establishment in South Africa of precisely the sort of regime which would be hostile to Western interests.

South Africa is now experiencing the 'pressure cooker' effect in the process of political change. The principal feature of this is the phenomenon of progressively rising aspirations. As soon as modest reforms are introduced, pressure by extremists increases and demand for more radical change is generated. The government is then faced with the choice of acceding to these demands at an ever increasing rate, which eventually accelerates outside their control and provokes a reactionary backlash; or of clamping down the lid of the pressure cooker, with the attendant risk of a violent explosion. The Shah of Iran, faced with a similar choice, took the first course, with the results which are now a matter of history.

The present phase in South Africa began in April 1981 when State President P. W. Botha and the Nationalist Party were elected on a mandate for political reform. In November 1983 the government submitted to a national referendum constitutional proposals designed to set up a new tricameral parliament consisting of a House of Assembly (white), a House of Representatives (coloured) and a House of Delegates (Indian). No provision was made for black participation. The referendum approved the new constitution, with 66 per cent of the (white) electorate in favour. The new parliament convened in September 1984 and held its first working session on 25 January 1985.

The reactions to the new structure were predictable. The extreme right, under Andries Treurnicht, protested that Botha was going too far, too fast. The black activists denounced the constitution as a sham. Serious unrest began to erupt, some of it specifically anti-white and anti-government, but some of it now directed against the coloured and Indian communities. There were, too, a number of appalling atrocities committed by blacks against black Africans suspected of 'collaborating with the government'.

An especially significant feature of the current unrest is the growing hostility between the communist-orientated African National Congress and the Inkatha of Chief Gatsha Buthulezi, the leader of Kwa Zulu. The Inkatha, which represents the powerful tribal influence of the Zulus, would clearly be an important element in any negotiated structure of power-sharing in South Africa; and the ANC has a vested interest in discouraging any such negotiations.

Faced with the unrest, the government declared a state of emergency. Although this has succeeded to some extent in containing the violence, there are still sporadic outbursts, some involving the Indian communities, who now regard themselves in many cases as being under threat from the black majority.

The declaration of the state of emergency also provided a stimulus for increased foreign pressures. Calls for economic sanctions and dis-investment were intensified, especially in the United States. A recent development was the speech of P. W. Botha to the National Party Congress of Natal in 1985. In his speech, the President outlined what he described as his manifesto for the future. He set the stage, apparently without preconditions, for negotiations to take place on the future political and constitutional structures in South Africa. At the same time he appeared to rule out the possibility of 'one man, one vote' in a unitary state; and he delivered a sombre warning to those engaged in violent protest.

President Botha has now clearly accepted that the pure doctrine of apartheid has failed. He is committed to negotiations aimed at power-sharing – a significant development in the policy of the National Party. He has accepted the principle of common citizenship in an undivided South Africa – he has, in effect, conceded most of the demands of moderate black leaders such as Gatsha Buthulezi.

One of the principal causes of disenchantment among Western critics is President Botha's failure to grant the unconditional release of Nelson Mandela, the imprisoned leader of the African National Congress. Although it seems reasonable enough to demand of a convicted terrorist, openly dedicated to the destruction of the South African political system, that he should refrain from violence if released, the conventional wisdom in the West is that, without Nelson Mandela, there can be no effective negotiations with the black majority. This is by no means self-evident since Mandela certainly would not speak for the Azanian People's Organization or for the Inkatha. He probably does not even command a clear majority in Soweto, his main power-base. Mandela can, in fact, claim to be a real leader only of the communists. Even so, it is likely that before too long some formula will be arrived at which will allow Mandela to take part in any future negotiation forum.

The widely accepted view, especially outside South Africa, is that there will be a progressive intensification of unrest and violence. Some observers believe that this will lead to the collapse of the white minority's will to govern and the early emergence of a black-dominated, one-party state on the Zimbabwe model. Others believe that the process will be more gradual and that the eventual overthrow of white rule will follow the emergence of a militant black middle class. Either way, most foreign observers seem to assume that the transfer of power to the black majority, by one means or another, sooner or later, is inevitable. It can be argued that they are mistaken. There are, indeed, at least two other possible scenarios.

One of these involves a descent into anarchy and civil war, with the withdrawal of the white minority into the traditional 'laager'. The other postulates continued white domination based upon overwhelming military strength, but with limited political participation by Indians, coloureds and blacks. Neither of these possibilities offers peace or freedom to all the people of South Africa; but, given the intransigence of the Afrikaaner and the implacable political ambitions of the black activists, peace with freedom in South Africa may not be a practical aspiration.

Much will depend on the actions of Western governments. If there is an intensive programme of sanctions and disinvestment, this will undoubtedly have a considerable impact on the South African economy. This will have its most dramatic effect on the standard of living of the black majority, and is therefore likely to be a catalyst for further violence. It is unlikely, however, to affect materially the policies of the South African government.

There are a number of important factors bearing upon any assessment of future developments in South Africa. The first is that the South African crisis is not a classical 'post-colonial' problem. The Afrikaaners, unlike the British and the Portuguese, have nowhere to go. Under one dispensation or another, their future is in South Africa. The second is that white South Africa is immensely strong. Although its economy has been temporarily destabilized, the underlying structure is sound. Militarily, South Africa is the most powerful nation in the continent. It has strong, efficient and loyal armed forces. It almost certainly has a nuclear weapon capability. It is capable of containing indefinitely any attempt at internal revolution and of withstanding any external threat short of attack by a superpower.

Black African opinion is by no means uniformly dedicated to the overthrow of the white government in Pretoria. Inside South Africa a substantial majority of blacks are probably in favour of peaceful change. The rest of black Africa would suffer severe economic effects if South Africa was destroyed or alienated. Most Western governments, while appreciating the importance of promoting human rights, recognize very clearly that they have a powerful vested interest, both economic and strategic, in the preservation of a strong and stable South Africa. They are unlikely, therefore, to give in readily to the fashionable demand for disinvestment and drastic economic sanctions.

It is possible to conclude that the 'bloodbath' or 'apocalypse' predicted (often by the people who would like to see an apocalyptic bloodbath) is in fact unlikely to take place. There will be violence and urban terrorism, sometimes of a frightening kind, in some areas of the country. The government is quite capable, however, of dealing with this. Some black leaders, notably Gatsha Buthulezi, are likely to react positively to the creation of any structure within which power-sharing can be negotiated. Other leaders will reject any attempt at peaceful change, since their aims and those of their sponsors are best served by anarchy and disintegration.

The most probable scenario for the immediate future is one in which the government of South Africa will continue to exercise effective control; in which there will be progressive dismantling of the discredited system of apartheid; and in which the best interests of the West will be served by encouraging progressive change rather than by pursuing punitive economic and diplomatic policies which risk creating a climate of collapse and disintegration.

CHAPTER ELEVEN

Central America and the Caribbean

It is a matter of profound importance for Britain and Western Europe that events in Central America and the Caribbean basin might soon bring about a significant shift in the centre of gravity of American foreign policy. Since the end of the Second World War, the main concentration of United States defence policy has been in the European–Atlantic area. The episodes in Korea and Vietnam were, to a very large extent, peripheral to the main concerns of American policy, which has been committed to preventing the expansion of Soviet power in Western Europe, and, by extension, into the North Atlantic, thus posing a threat to the American homeland.

The emergence of a serious Soviet threat in Latin America is perceived by some American strategists as a more immediate danger. At the same time, there has been a growing disenchantment with Europe in the minds of many influential Americans. The inability of Western Europe to formulate anything remotely resembling a common foreign policy or strategic doctrine, coupled with a tendency in Europe to be instinctively critical of American foreign policy, has led to a sense of irritation and frustration, and to a questioning of the value of the 'entangling Alliance'.

Out of this has emerged a concept sometimes described as 'global unilateralism', an American foreign policy in which there would be no formal and general alliances, but a series of *ad hoc* arrangements, designed to protect and further specifically American interests, concluded with powers or groups of powers prepared to recognize those interests and make common cause with the United States in defending them. One of these interests is, quite clearly, the stability of Latin America and the Caribbean. Many European allies seem unable or unwilling to recognize this, accusing the United States of exaggerating the threat and interfering in the internal affairs of sovereign states. It is therefore not surprising that American policy-makers should concern themselves with cultivating potential allies in the region. The conflicts of interest arising from this became very clear at the time of Britain's war with Argentina over the Falkland Islands.

The American perception of the nature of the threat was set out in February 1982 in testimony by a State Department official before the Senate Foreign Relations Committee and the House Foreign Affairs Committee.[65] Cuba was systematically expanding its capacity to project military power beyond its shores, employing the largest air, land and naval forces in the region. Nicaragua was being exploited as a base for the export of subversion and armed intervention throughout Central America, with nearly 2000 Soviet, East European and Cuban advisers in place. More recently the United States government had accused Nicaragua of giving shelter and support to international terrorist groups from all over the world. Meanwhile, the decisive battle for Central America was under way in El Salvador; and an acute economic crisis afflicted the whole of the Caribbean basin.

The Soviet interest in this strategically important area is obvious. However, since its humiliating reverse in the Cuba missile crisis of 1962, it has adopted a low profile in the region, concentrating on maintaining support for its client state in the area, Cuba. The advent of the Sandinistas in Nicaragua in 1979 provided a second base for Soviet influence in the area, and the Soviet government immediately embarked on a programme of economic and military assistance to the Sandinista government. According to two regional observers, 'the Nicaraguan pattern of rapid revolutionary transformation and Soviet involvement in the early 1980s is very reminiscent of the Cuban pattern in the early 1960s.'[66] The long-term Soviet policy is, as Dr Harold Blakemore, Secretary of the Institute of Latin American Studies at the University of London, has pointed out, 'to create conditions favourable to the advancement of its global interests close to the US, and to rely upon the latter's policies to aid that objective, namely, to count upon internal dissent within the United States itself, and a growing concern that those policies are not really conducive to Western interests in the region as a whole.'[67]

The American reaction to these developments has been predictable. It is the traditional policy of the United States government that no power – and particularly no non-regional power – should be permitted to threaten perceived national interests on the US borders or in the oceans around the United States. This attitude was enshrined in the Monroe Doctrine of 1823, a unilateral declaration, with no basis in international law, which has been underwritten by American power ever since.

Soviet support for Cuba, and specifically the Cuba missile crisis of 1962, led to a clearly defined American policy designed to resist the further spread of Russian power in the area. The growing crisis in the region came to a head with the overthrow of General Somoza in Nicaragua and the assumption of power in 1979 by the Sandinistas – an overtly Marxist political movement. This met with open hostility from the United States, which provided substantial aid for anti-Sandinista guerrilla groups – the Contras; and from 1980 onwards the crisis in the area has progressively intensified until it has become an obvious flashpoint for a conflict which would clearly extend beyond Central America itself. The Contadora Group – Mexico, Venezuela, Colombia and Panama – was set up as a consultative body in 1983 in an attempt to mediate in the crisis. The Contadora objectives, which have been accepted by all parties, include an end to support for cross-border subversion and destabilization of Central American governments; an end to the arms race and foreign military bases and advisers; elimination of the traffic in arms; full pluralist democracy; and respect for human rights. There have been four main stages in the Contadora process, each an elaboration of the preceding one.

Between January and July 1983 a communiqué was issued by the Foreign Ministers at the conclusion of their meeting on the island of Contadora, appealing to the countries of Central America to work for a reduction of tension through dialogue and negotiation and to establish a framework for peaceful coexistence between them. In July there was a meeting in Cancun of the Presidents of the four Contadora countries, who issued a declaration calling for peaceful negotiation.

In September 1983 there was agreement between four Contadora countries and the five Central American states (Costa Rica, El Salvador, Guatemala, Honduras and Nicaragua) on a Document of Objectives. In January 1984, the Contadora and the Central American states agreed on a document listing specific measures to be taken to fulfil the commitments implied by the Document of Objectives. Since then there has been a period of drafting and negotiation of the Contadora Act for Peace and Cooperation in Central America.

Meanwhile, in October 1983, there occurred an event which provided a classic case history in crisis management. In Grenada, the most southerly of the Windward Islands in the Caribbean, Mr Maurice Bishop, the Prime Minister, was overthrown and killed in a coup staged by a rival factor of the ruling party – the New Jewel Movement – which had been in power since 1979. A few days after the formation of a new government, a force of United States Marines and parachute troops, together with a small contingent of troops from neighbouring Caribbean states, landed on the island and established military authority within a few days after overcoming resistance by the Grenada People's Revolutionary Army and a number of Cuban workers. Sir Paul Scoon, the Grenada Governor-General, who had requested foreign assistance after the death of Mr Bishop, then formed an Advisory Council to exercise power until elections could be held.

The case for American intervention, in the context of the Monroe Doctrine and of the security of the United States, was a strong one. Under its military government, Grenada was even more clearly in the Soviet sphere of influence than it had been under Mr Bishop. There was a large Cuban presence on the island, much of it military; there were Soviet military advisers, and a second airport, capable of taking Soviet military transports, was being built by Cuban workers, although the existing airport is more than adequate for Grenada's modest tourist trade. Grenada was seen by the neighbouring Caribbean states as posing a threat to their own stability.

The island had become a Soviet-dominated base suitable for destabilizing Venezuela and Colombia to the south; and since Grenada is a thousand miles closer than Havana to Libya and Angola, it would have been able to provide a valuable staging post for arms destined for Nicaragua and El Salvador. The Brazilian government had, indeed, recently halted a Libyan aircraft carrying arms to Central America labelled as agricultural implements. The prompt and effective American military action, however, did not meet with universal acclaim by the allies of the United States.

In the British press there was considerable resentment that the United States had 'invaded' a country of which the Queen of England was the constitutional head, an attitude which led Mrs Jeane Kirkpatrick, the United States Permanent Representative at the United Nations, to make the significant comment that the American government could not 'give our allies a veto power over our national security'. The Commonwealth Secretary-General and the United Nations General Assembly, predictably, called for the withdrawal of American troops. By the middle of December, all American forces had, in fact, withdrawn, handing over security to troops of the Caribbean states. On 3 December 1984, a general election was held, and the House of Representatives met for the first time since 1979, when it had been suspended by the New Jewel Movement. The New National Party, a conservative grouping, won fourteen of the fifteen seats and formed a government.

Some of America's European allies seem disinclined to recognize the threats to the stability of the region. The French government in the course of a visit by President Mitterrand to Mexico in 1983 had recognized the main guerrilla movement in El Salvador (the Farabundo Marti Movement of National Liberation – FMLN), together with its political wing, as 'representative political forces'. The Dutch government made a similar declaration. On the other hand, the Foreign Affairs Committee of the British House of Commons published a detailed report on Central America and the Caribbean[68] in which it urged Nicaragua to abandon its policy of exploiting revolution, and the United States to mitigate its hostility towards the Sandinista regime.

It is arguable, however, that the confrontation has now gone so far that this kind of exhortation represents no more than a pious hope.

If the crisis is to be resolved successfully, some way has to be found to reconcile American fears about the threat to its strategic interests in the area with a recognition of the social and economic pressures that undoubtedly exist. On the one hand, it may be true, as one Latin American observer has written, that 'the United States will only succeed as a hegemonic power normally does, if it considers these countries for what they are, not for fear of what the Soviet Union may do, and if it values these countries for themselves, not as pawns in a chess game with the USSR.'[69] On the other hand, the Soviet threat to the region is real, and those regional governments which are willing to be pawns of the USSR should not complain too loudly if they are treated as such. They do, after all, live in a region in which United States power is paramount.

CHAPTER TWELVE

———◆———

China and Hong Kong

It is a statement of the obvious to say that China is emerging as one of the great powers of the world, with its vast geographical area and massive population now being developed by a pragmatic and dynamic leadership. China has set itself the task of quadrupling the value of its annual industrial and agricultural output by the end of the century. In pursuit of this staggeringly ambitious aim, the Third Plenum of the 12th National Party Congress endorsed plans to revitalize Chinese industry and to accelerate the process of modernization in such areas as industry, agriculture, science and technology – and eventually in the People's Liberation Army, a national defence force of over 4 million men and women.

The recent developments in Chinese government thinking have given rise to some characteristically crass comments in certain sections of the Western press. China, we have been told by various solemn commentators, is going capitalist. This is something of an over-simplification. It is true to say, however, that what is happening in China is a further sign that the Chinese are positioning themselves to live on equal terms in the international community with the great capitalist economies of the West.

For this reason alone, it is essential that the United Kingdom should nourish and develop its relations with the People's Republic. But there is a more specific motivation as well – the imperatives of common interests in the geopolitical and strategic sphere. The growing strength of Soviet military power and the persistent readiness of the USSR to use it in pursuit of expansionist foreign policies has already been discussed. It is relevant, however, to concentrate for a moment on one aspect of Russian military policy – its growing strength in North-East Asia.

On 17 September 1985, the US Japan Advisory Commission published a report on the Soviet build-up. It underlined the recent modernization of Soviet forces in the area, confirming the belief, held for some time in Western intelligence circles, that the Pacific Fleet is now the most important formation in the Soviet Navy, with 125 submarines, 30 of them armed with ballistic missiles. There are 135 SS20 missiles and 70 Backfire bombers, all, of course, with nuclear capability, deployed in North-East Asia. The Soviet Union does not develop and deploy its vast military potential without specific strategic and geopolitical reasons. It is clear that the Soviet Union has concluded, in common with many Western strategists and economists, that the centre of gravity of global power is moving progressively from the European–Atlantic area to the Pacific Basin; and the Russians, who understand as well as anyone the role of military power in foreign policy, have laid their plans accordingly. Where, then, does China stand in all this? In general the Chinese analysis of Russian global strategy is remarkably similar to the consensus among Western strategists. It postulates an ultimate aim of world supremacy, by way of the progressive separation of Western Europe from the United States, the neutralization of America, the Finlandization of Europe, and the eventual drive to the East. Yet the Chinese would be the first to admit that their own armed forces have certain limitations. Their equipment is in need of modernization; their defensive strategy is based on the concept of the People's War, envisaging the swallowing up of invading forces in the vast areas of the Chinese heartland; and it has a long-standing and recently reiterated policy of 'no first use' of nuclear weapons.

The conclusion from this must be that the West has a clear interest in the emergence of a defensively strong China. This is not to suggest anything so simplistic as a military alliance, which, in present circumstances, would be unwelcome to the Chinese anyway. This does not rule out, however, increasing collaboration at the diplomatic and military staff level; and it would certainly make sense for the West to give every assistance to China in building up modern, highly trained defence forces, equipped with the kind of modern weapons and military technology which it needs to deter the Soviet Union from any military adventures in Asia.

It is in this context, then, that we have to consider future relations between this country and the People's Republic; and we have an appropriate point of departure in the agreement recently arrived at on the future of Hong Kong. It is an agreement which has produced reactions ranging from something approaching euphoria in some quarters through the equivocal judgment that it is 'the best of a bad job' to the somewhat sour judgment that it is an almost unmitigated abdication of British responsibility. Before attempting to assess where the truth possibly lies, it might be as well to dispose of one area of confusion.

There was no alternative to some kind of negotiated agreement with China. Of the three relevant treaties, it is true, two granted territory to Britain *in perpetuity* – the Treaty of Nanking in 1842 for the island of Hong Kong, and the Convention of Peking in 1860 for South Kowloon and Stonecutters Island – but over 90 per cent of the territory of Hong Kong, the so-called New Territories, was ceded for ninety-nine years in 1898, and will automatically revert to China in 1997. There was never, except in the minds of a small number of incurable optimists, the remotest chance that China would agree to an extension of the 1898 Convention; or to any ideas of transfer and lease-back. Nor was there any realistic possibility of maintaining Hong Kong Island and South Kowloon as a viable entity in isolation from the New Territories.

Those isolated voices that compared Hong Kong with the Falkland Islands and muttered about the Royal Navy and the SAS were simply not living in the real world. An agreement there had to be; the only question was, how good an agreement.

The considered opinion must be that it has provided, insofar as it is within the power of governments to do so, safeguards for the future of Hong Kong of a kind which few people can have expected when the negotiations began. It is not necessary, even if there were time, to rehearse the provisions of the agreement in detail. Briefly, it has been agreed that sovereignty over Hong Kong will be resumed by China from 1 July 1997.

From that date, Hong Kong will become a Special Administrative Region (SAR), as provided in the provisions of Article 31 of the Chinese

Constitution. The Hong Kong SAR will enjoy a high degree of autonomy in its domestic affairs; foreign and defence matters will be the responsibilities of China. Hong Kong will be vested with executive, legislative and independent judicial power, including that of final adjudication. The laws currently in force will remain basically unchanged.

The present social and economic system in Hong Kong will continue, and so will the lifestyle. Rights and freedoms, including those of the person, of speech, of the press, of assembly, of association, of travel, of movement, of correspondence, of strike, of choice of occupation, of academic research and religious belief will be ensured. Private property, right of inheritance and foreign investments will be protected.

Hong Kong will retain the status of a free port, a separate customs territory and an international financial centre. Foreign exchange, gold, securities and futures markets will continue. The Hong Kong dollar will continue to circulate and remain freely convertible. There will be no exchange controls, and the free flow of capital will be allowed. Hong Kong will manage its own finances: China will not levy any taxes in the Hong Kong SAR.

Hong Kong will be allowed to maintain and develop economic and cultural relations and to conclude relevant agreements with other foreign countries and international organizations. Hong Kong will also issue its own travel documents.

The above rights and privileges will be incorporated in the Basic Law of Hong Kong by the National People's Congress and they will remain unchanged for fifty years. To ensure a smooth transfer, a Sino-British Joint Liaison Group will be set up in 1988.

Although the full details of the negotiations will not be known for some time, it is possible to speculate that, in arriving at this agreement, both sides made substantial concessions. The major concession from Britain was inevitable. It was to give up any idea of retaining sovereignty, even over Hong Kong Island, and also any idea of continuing to administer any part of the territory after 1997. The Chinese concessions were to the British demands for a fully detailed document, legally binding and going much further than pious statements of intent; and to a delay to defuse any impression of an immediate *de facto* takeover by China or any pre-emptive interference in the internal affairs of Hong Kong.

Whether the agreement is fully acceptable to the Chinese government is a matter which only they can answer. They have initialled it, and it is clearly not subject to renegotiation. A more relevant problem for the United Kingdom is whether the agreement is satisfactory for this country and the people of Hong Kong. Before the agreement was reached the Unofficial Members of the Executive and Legislative Councils (UMELCO) published a paper in May 1986 in which they set out four basic requirements which were considered to be essential if the agreement were to be acceptable to the people of Hong Kong.

These were, first, that the agreement must contain full details of all the systems in Hong Kong after 1997; second, that it must state that the provisions of the Basic Law will incorporate the relevant positions of the agreement; third, that it must provide adequate and workable assurances that the terms of the agreement will be honoured; and, finally, that the rights of the Hong Kong British nationals will be safeguarded.

These requirements have been, to a remarkable degree, met by the agreement. It provides as much detail as could reasonably be expected about Chinese intentions after 1997; it states that future Basic Law will enshrine the provisions of the agreement in a legally binding document which is the highest form of commitment between two sovereign states; and the existing rights and freedoms of the people of Hong Kong are guaranteed. The only area about which there may be residual doubts is that which concerns the national status and rights of the Hong Kong Chinese; and there is, of course, much disappointment at the decision that after 1997 Hong Kong British nationals will no longer be able to pass on their right to use British passports to their children.

The immediate impression is of a remarkably successful agreement, and one which reinforces the foundations of continuing prosperity in Hong Kong; and it would be ungracious not to acknowledge the very considerable achievement of those who so patiently negotiated. They did so in the face of many difficulties, including the pressures of an insatiable press corps who were seemingly unable to believe the evidence of their senses – that an important international negotiation was actually being conducted confidentially, and not through a series of inspired leaks and indiscretions.

Why, then, is everyone still not entirely satisfied? It would be foolish to deny that many people are saying, 'Yes, the agreement is all right as far as it goes, but how do we know it will be honoured?'

There are a number of answers to that question. The first is that the agreement is the highest form of binding commitment between two sovereign states; and the record of China in honouring its international commitments will bear comparison with that of the rest of the international community. But, of course, there is a limit to which, in practice as opposed to theory, a government can bind its successors; and there are those who point to a recent history of turbulence and unpredictability in the Chinese political structure; others express doubts about the Chinese ability to manage a capitalist economy, of which few Chinese leaders have much experience; still others fear that after 1997 mainland Chinese will resent the special status of Hong Kong SAR and press for restrictions on its free market economy. For many, it is simply impossible to conceive of half a century of viability for a free-wheeling, brash and extravagant capitalist enclave within the collectivist system of the People's Republic.

Much will depend on the way in which China handles its approach to the Joint Liaison Group – especially in such matters as freedom of movement after 1997. The Chinese can do much to reassure the people of Hong Kong.

All this underlines the importance of future relations between Britain and China. It is those relations which will, in the long run, dictate the survivability of the Hong Kong agreement. In the present climate, China has no conceivable interest in damaging the prosperity and stability of Hong Kong. It must be the aim of both countries to ensure that this state of affairs persists. Britain, together with its allies in the United States and the EEC, must collaborate with China in such a way that the People's Republic becomes so involved in the commercial, economic and strategic concerns of the outside world that it is never again driven, or tempted, back into isolation.

In Britain we have a special role and a special opportunity. If it is to achieve its goal of an economic and industrial revolution in fifteen years, China needs the cooperation of this country, which has very special skills and talents to offer. One of the basic engines of the Chinese modernization programme will be energy supply. It will need to develop its coal and oil resources; to expand its supplies of natural gas; to develop hydroelectric and alternative energy sources; and to engage in an ambitious programme of nuclear energy generation. Britain is already involved in the construction of a nuclear plant with two 900-megaton pressurized water reactors in Guandong Province – in collaboration with Hong Kong. This is only one example of the opportunities which will exist in the future for British industry, science and technology.

There is an almost unique opportunity, in the aftermath of the Hong Kong agreement, for Britain to develop and expand a special relationship with China, not only in the industrial field, but in the spheres of diplomacy and grand strategy. The common interests of our two countries are self-evident. There is a tendency, however, among the British to concern themselves too much with the internal political systems of other countries and not enough with their own vital, and common, strategic and political interests.

It is not only Britain and China who can shape a common future. As Michael Sandberg, Chairman of the Hong Kong Bank, said in a speech in London in 1985, 'We can see a rapidly modernizing China which, although anxious not to turn its back on recent history too ostentatiously, is a China which nevertheless fully recognizes the advantages to itself of a more open economy and society.' In that context, he said, significantly, 'The principal question becomes not what will China do *to* Hong Kong, but what can Hong Kong do *for* China?'

We should now move into a new phase of Anglo-Chinese relations, based upon a realization of the changing geopolitical environment in which the global centre of gravity is shifting towards the Pacific; upon a shared appreciation of our common strategic and economic concerns; and upon the foundation of trust and civilized communication characterized by the Hong Kong agreement. From our strong position in the Western Alliance and the EEC we should take the lead in developing and expanding the relationships between China and the West as a whole.

It would, however, be appropriate to add a word of caution. Too often British businessmen and industrialists have bustled off to China, expecting to conclude great deals and finalize mammoth projects in a few weeks or even days. The Chinese are a careful, austere and thrifty people. They are tough negotiators and they have a number of idiosyncrasies which Western businessmen find unfamiliar – for example, they believe you should not borrow money unless you have a reasonable certainty of paying it back; and, above all, the Chinese do not understand our obsessive desire to conclude negotiations, however complicated the issue, in a few days of hectic bargaining. They have, after all, an historic time-frame which is somewhat different from ours.

With patience on both sides, cooperation and friendship between Britain and China can enter a new dimension and have a substantial influence on the way the world will look in the twenty-first century.

PART THREE

Britain's Role and Responsibilities

CHAPTER THIRTEEN

—•—

Britain, NATO and Nuclear Strategy

Of all the global crisis areas considered so far there is none, with the possible exception of Gibraltar, in which the United Kingdom might be expected to act unilaterally in any attempt at military intervention. The possibility of some 'repeat performance' of the Falklands episode is expressly excluded. It can be argued that this was an aberration brought about by a conjunction of circumstances in which an irrational and doomed military adventure by an Argentinian military government was encouraged by a series of misunderstandings, misappreciations and political confusion in this country. The situation was restored by resolute, well-planned military action. It is unlikely, however, to recur. Only through some machinery of collective security might Britain be expected to bring any significant influence to bear in the main strategic pressure centres of the world. This has clear implications for the formulation of British defence policy.

It is true that France and Britain still accept certain responsibilities outside Europe, specifically in regard to their overseas territories and their former colonies, including those in the Caribbean Basin. However, the other European members of NATO regard themselves, for the most part, as states whose security interests are restricted to the European–Atlantic area. This is not to say that these Western European countries have no interest in global security, but, as one authoritative West German observer has written, 'They are not prepared to accept military responsibilities outside the North Atlantic Treaty area.'[70]

This reluctance on the part of NATO and of most of its constituent states to consider seriously the threat posed by crises 'out of area' severely inhibits the ability of the Alliance and its members to influence the course of events in some of the areas of potential crisis. Central America, the Caribbean Basin and Equatorial and Southern Africa all lie south of the Tropic of Cancer and are thus legally (and practically) outside the scope of collective action. In the other areas there are substantial differences of approach among member nations. Nevertheless, there can be no effective crisis management in any of the areas under study without effective consultation, communication and contingency planning.

So far as British policy is concerned, the principles have been clearly enunciated in successive statements on the Defence Estimates. Exports account for some 30 per cent of Britain's gross domestic product. Britain therefore has a strong interest in seeing peace and stability maintained in the country's trading partners; in securing the supplies of oil and strategic minerals that are vital to national security. In pursuit of these interests it maintains its worldwide programme of military deployments and exercises. However, as a recent White Paper has made clear, 'Our aim in the first instance must be to bring diplomatic and economic efforts to bear in the areas of potential instability so as to help maintain peace and combat the activities of the Soviet Union and its proxies.'[71] The British government, however, regards itself also as capable of intervening militarily, 'either alone or in concert with our allies', to defend British interests. The capability to undertake intervention of this kind is being constantly enhanced.

British armed forces are also expected to contribute to the preservation of regional stability by military assistance programmes. Britain has about 1000 servicemen on loan to foreign countries or helping to train students from over seventy non-NATO countries. The principal capacity to act outside the NATO area is based, however, on selected units whose primary roles are within the Alliance but which can be deployed rapidly at long range in a crisis. Such deployment would inevitably leave gaps in the defences of NATO. The policy of the British government is to 'maintain our effective intervention capability and to reaffirm our willingness to help defend Western interest outside the NATO area'. It would be unwise, however, to overestimate Britain's capacity, in the face of domestic economic and political pressures, for engaging in large-scale crisis management especially outside the NATO area.

However it was Lenin who said in a speech in 1920: 'As long as capitalism and socialism exist, we cannot live in peace: in the end one or the other will triumph – a funeral dirge will be sung over the Soviet republic or over world capitalism'; and it is in the context of this prophecy that Britain has to deal with the many-faceted threat to its security.

Like any other advanced industrial country in the West, Britain must clearly ensure that it is able to deter a potential enemy from *any* course of military action that would threaten its own national security. History has so far shown no way of achieving this without the possession of the classic deterrent against military attack – an effective and credible military defence. Hitherto, there has been a large measure of consensus in our society and its political establishment about how the military defence of a medium-sized industrial nation like Britain should be organized.

Britain is, and has been for most of its history, primarily a 'European' nation. Even at the height of British imperial power, Britain's political concerns and preoccupations were involved more with Europe than with the Empire. Now that the days of the Empire are over, Britain has returned more formally to the European role in which it has always been more at ease. British culture is strongly European and, as Roy Jenkins, a former British Cabinet minister, has pointed out, most of Britain's diplomatic efforts have traditionally been devoted to maintaining our interests among the shifting sands of European politics; and it has been in European wars that Britain has periodically committed its national effort. 'It is Blenheim, Waterloo and the Somme which are the great remembered battles of British history, not Plassey or Omdurman or even Yorktown.'[72]

It is often suggested that Britain's position in the world power structure lies at the intersection of three circles – Europe, the Atlantic and the Commonwealth. This view, which has contributed to the misleading conception of Britain as the third great world power after the United States and the Soviet Union, is based upon at least one notable fallacy – the significance of the Commonwealth. This strange conglomeration of disparate and often hostile nations has nothing in common beyond the fact that its members were once under British rule. It has no political or economic coherence and, although some people in the United Kingdom are still reluctant to recognize the fact, it provides for Britain no basis for any special role in world affairs. Indeed, it can be argued that overpreoccupation with the susceptibilities of the 'new Commonwealth' has often caused Britain to neglect its real strategic and political interests.

Britain's place is at the conjunction of European and American spheres of interest and influence. For some time there has been a struggle for predominance in the formulation of British foreign policy between those who believe that the American or Atlantic element should be pre-eminent, and those who see Western Europe, with Britain as a fully committed member state, emerging as a third power, to stand alongside the two superpowers in the world's political structure. It has frequently been argued that the absence of Britain from the Messina Conference which led directly to the Treaty of Rome and the establishment of the European Economic Community was a grave error of foreign policy; and when Britain eventually acceded to the Community in 1973, it was widely assumed that Britain's future lay unequivocally with Europe.

Unhappily, the EEC has, so far, dismally failed to realize its potential as a political organization. It has had only limited success in harmonizing its foreign policies. Confronted with an international crisis of any kind, the instinct of the member countries of the Community is to consult their own national interests first and only then, somewhat reluctantly, to address themselves to the collective concerns of Western Europe. Members of the EEC thus frequently find themselves in direct conflict with each other in their approaches to crises in international relations.

The principal vehicle of Britain's approach to collective security in the West is therefore not the European Community, but the North Atlantic Treaty Organization; and here, too, Britain occupies a distinctive position. It is the only member of the integrated military structure of the Alliance to possess nuclear weapons. Those nuclear weapons are dedicated primarily to support of Alliance strategies and are included in the targeting plans of the American Supreme Allied Commander.

The result of all this is that Britain has been, in the past, inclined to attach itself more closely, in strategic terms, to the American or Atlantic pillar of the Alliance than to the European. Britain is, in fact, a medium-sized power, with a strategic nuclear weapons capability, which bases its military policies upon its membership of the North Atlantic Treaty Organization and its foreign policies substantially upon a 'special relationship' with the United States of America. It is from this point of departure that any analysis of the British role in contemporary international affairs has to begin.

The consequence is that Britain's military resources are substantially committed to the defence of the European–Atlantic area, although, unlike most of its European allies, it still has small forces deployed in potential crisis areas elsewhere in the world. There are detachments, mainly all-arms groups supporting an infantry battalion, in Belize, Brunei, Cyprus, the Falkland Islands and Gibraltar. A larger force of about 8000 is in Hong Kong and another of nearly 10,000 in Northern Ireland. The main British military force, however, is in the Federal Republic of Germany where there is an infantry corps of 56,000 troops supported by 10,000 Royal Air Force, and capable of rapid reinforcement from the United Kingdom, designed to bring the total up to 150,000. The United Kingdom also provides 70 per cent of the ready NATO maritime forces dedicated to the task of safeguarding the reinforcement and resupply routes through the eastern Atlantic and Channel areas.

The British government, however, recognizes that 'despite our best efforts and those of our friends and allies, deterrence can fail and situations arise in which we have no option but to intervene militarily to defend our legitimate interests.'[73] Accordingly, in addition to the garrisons permanently deployed outside the NATO area, Britain maintains an Airborne Brigade capable of delivering a parachute force of battalion strength in a single assault. A second battalion is in the process of being trained and equipped for this role, and the British capability for the distant projection of modest but effective military force is being gradually enhanced, although it is unlikely to approach that of France, which maintains a Rapid Action Force of almost 50,000 men organized into several divisions. In addition to the Airborne Brigade a Royal Marine Commando Brigade, which has a primary role on NATO's northern flank, is also earmarked for operations 'out of area'.

The basis of any contemporary British defence policy must, however, be collective security, based upon the assumption that an alliance of like-minded nations is able to offer a more effective defence than a number of individual states which could be picked off separately by a determined enemy. Britain has rightly chosen therefore to maintain full membership of the North Atlantic Treaty Organization. To this alliance it makes a significant contribution, both to conventional defence and to nuclear deterrence. A substantial section of the European theatre of operations is defended by British Army and Air Force units, while the security of the communication routes across the Atlantic is partly the responsibility of the Royal Navy. Indeed, apart from those special garrisons and detachments in such places as Northern Ireland, the Falkland Islands, Hong Kong and Gibraltar, Britain's conventional forces are allocated to, and fully integrated within, the North Atlantic Treaty Organization. Although they have certain critical deficiencies of strength, deployment and equipment, they constitute an important and indispensable element of the conventional defences of the Alliance.

They are, however, like the rest of NATO's forces in Europe, attempting to implement a defensive strategy for which they are neither organized nor equipped. A certain prescription for disaster is to base national or collective security upon a carefully constructed military strategy, and then persistently fail to provide the resources necessary to implement it. For this reason the ability of NATO to implement the defensive-deterrent doctrine, generally described as flexible or graduated response, has for some time been regarded with considerable reservation by a substantial body of opinion – not only among professional planners and military commanders but also among academic strategists.

Perhaps the most articulate and authoritative advocate of more realistic approaches to the defence of Western Europe is General Bernard Rogers, until recently Supreme Allied Commander Europe, who has raised to an almost evangelical level his campaign to exploit Western technological superiority in order to offset the numerical superiority of the Warsaw Pact and so improve the deterrent posture of NATO's defensive forces. He proceeds from an assumption that the doctrine of flexible response is entirely valid, provided that the resources necessary to implement it are clearly available. The validity of this doctrine depends upon the concept of controlled escalation, in which any attack by the Warsaw Pact forces would be met at each stage by an appropriately graduated reaction, including the use of 'battlefield' or 'tactical' nuclear weapons if it proved impossible to contain the enemy advance by conventional means. This has involved the forward deployment of a considerable number of low-yield nuclear weapons to implement the first stages of the process of escalation, and, by extension, to provide a manifest deterrent against an attack with even limited objectives.

This doctrine has always, of course, implied a readiness by NATO forces to use nuclear weapons first; and it is in this context that most of the doubts about its credibility have arisen. Many serious analysts have insisted that, as tactical or battlefield nuclear weapons are for all practical purposes under ultimate American control, their first use against a conventional attack would be extremely unlikely, since there would be no guarantee of a similarly limited Soviet response. In the language of the more trenchant critics, no President of the United States is likely to put New York or Chicago at risk to preserve the integrity of the European theatre of operations. The counter-argument has been that no leader of the Soviet Union could ever be sure of this, and that the inevitable doubts about American reaction are in themselves an effective deterrent. As General Rogers insists, even with adequate conventional capabilities, NATO could never be *certain* of defeating a conventional attack without escalation; removing the element of uncertainty from the mind of a potential aggressor, for example by declaring a 'no first use' policy, would therefore seriously weaken the nuclear deterrent.

The Warsaw Pact, however, has always been able to outrange NATO's 'battlefield' nuclear weapons with its conventional artillery. As Dr Manfred Woerner, Defence Minister of the Federal Republic of Germany, pointed out in May 1982, 60 per cent of the American nuclear weapons in Europe have a range of less than thirty kilometres and the great majority of these weapons have a range of under fifteen kilometres. 'This means nothing more and nothing less than that the greater range of Soviet tube and rocket artillery presents the opportunity for the Warsaw Pact, under many battle conditions, to destroy by conventional means NATO's nuclear insertion capability, while its own weapons are beyond the effective range of NATO forces.' The equation has been further complicated by significant improvements in the nuclear capability of the Soviet Union. The strategy of flexible response was developed over a period of fifteen years during which the United States possessed a clear degree of nuclear superiority.

It was estimated in 1952 that the conventional defence of Western Europe required force levels of 96 divisions and 9000 aircraft to pose a credible response to the powerful ground forces of the Warsaw Pact. In the political and economic climate of postwar Europe these levels (the so-called 'Lisbon Goals') were clearly unrealistic, and even a compromise plan for 50 divisions and 4000 aircraft had no prospect of being achieved.

By 1956 NATO had decided to settle for 26 divisions and 1400 aircraft. These demonstrably inadequate conventional forces were to act as a 'trip wire', designed to trigger off American nuclear retaliation against nuclear attack. It was planned to deploy 15,000 'tactical' nuclear weapons which were to be, in effect, an extension of conventional firepower. It was still the *strategic* superiority of the United States which was to provide a nuclear umbrella of extended deterrence for Western Europe. In the event only 7000 battlefield nuclear weapons were deployed, and in 1967 NATO adopted its strategy of flexible response, which postulated a significant improve-

ment in conventional forces – an improvement which never material-
ized. Theory and fact therefore failed to coincide. There was, in fact,
no capacity for flexible response – the security of Western Europe
continued to rely upon a form of massive retaliation, which, so far as
it has ever made sense at all, did so only in the context of decisive
American nuclear superiority.

In the meantime, that superiority has virtually disappeared. As Sam
Nunn, the United States Senator from Georgia, pointed out in 1982
in the course of his testimony to the Senate Armed Services Committee:

> By attaining strategic nuclear parity with the United States, the
> Soviet Union has severely undermined the credibility of US
> strategic nuclear forces as a deterrent to a conventional attack
> on Europe.

It is not too extreme to suggest that a strategy of flexible response, if
widely perceived to be incapable of implementation, carries with it
dangers which might eventually threaten the disintegration of the
Western Alliance. So long as NATO relies upon defensive resources
which allow virtually *no* flexibility and no range of options between
retreat and nuclear retaliation (between 'suicide and surrender'), there
is a very real danger that, in a crisis, the West might be forced to submit to military blackmail; and the growing public awareness of these
dangers is beginning to cause severe political problems in several
NATO countries, especially in the light of recent discussions between
the United States and the Soviet Union on the possible removal of all
intermediate-range nuclear missiles from Europe.

Yet the obvious alternatives present their own dangers and difficulties. To return to the declared policy of massive retaliation, in the
current state of the strategic nuclear balance, would obviously lack all
credibility; while to attempt to match Russian conventional strength
by building up NATO's own conventional forces to an adequate level
is as unrealistic, politically and economically, as it was at the time of
the Lisbon Goals. A new conceptual approach to the defence of
Western Europe is clearly essential; and in this context modern tech-

nology offers remarkable possibilities for the strengthening of conventional striking power without substantial numerical increases in forces and equipment.

An important aim of British defence policy must therefore be to maintain, and eventually to improve, the strength of its contribution to the conventional defence of Western Europe. In due course of time it should be possible to redeploy to Europe the military resources at present committed to non-NATO tasks in Northern Ireland, the South Atlantic and Hong Kong. At the same time, developments in information technology and precision-guided munitions will make it possible to enhance the defensive capability of the British Army of the Rhine without the need for substantial increases in the number of troops deployed, a measure which would certainly involve a return to some form of compulsory military service. Although this might be desirable on both social and military grounds, it is unlikely that a British government of any complexion would regard it as politically feasible.

The debate on these issues is taking place against a background of significant changes in the pattern of international relations as well as in the technology of war. The United States, Britain's major NATO ally, is beginning to re-examine its own strategic assumptions in a way which might well weaken its present commitment to policies based on the defence of the European–Atlantic area. Threats to American national interests are perceived in Central America, where the expansion of Soviet influence and the consequent destabilization of the region is beginning to pose a direct threat to the mainland United States. At the same time the geopolitical and economic centre of gravity is beginning to shift from the European–Atlantic area to the Pacific Basin. Faced with these changes in the strategic calculus, the mood of 'global unilateralism' is emerging in the United States. It is composed of a recognition of the global nature of the threat to the free world, together with a sense of frustration brought about by the inevitable problems of Alliance politics.

As a result, the United States administration, and the American people, are becoming increasingly impatient with European allies who seem to expect the United States to bear the largest burden of the defence of the free world, but who are openly unsympathetic and un-supportive when the United States is faced with a crisis elsewhere in the world – or 'out of area', as the NATO planners describe it. Developments in military science and technology are, at the same time, beginning to undermine all the familiar certainties about military strategy whether nuclear or conventional. The possibilities reflected in space-based anti-missile defence, precision-guided weapons, directed-energy and kinetic-energy weapons and lasers are rapidly transforming the strategic environment.

CHAPTER FOURTEEN

The Significance of 'Star Wars'

The question of ballistic missile defence has always been central to any serious debate about nuclear strategy, deterrence and arms control. Four years ago, however, it entered a new dimension; and it now has a direct and important relevance for British defence planning.

On 23 March 1983, President Reagan announced in a television broadcast that he was 'directing a comprehensive and intensive effort to define long-term research and development programmes to begin to achieve our ultimate goal of eliminating the threat posed by strategic nuclear missiles . . . this would pave the way for arms control measures to eliminate the weapons themselves.' Subsequently, after preliminary investigations had suggested that research might prove that strategic defence of this kind was feasible, the President established a Strategic Defence Initiative Office (SDIO) under Lieutenant General James A. Abrahamson to implement the research programme.

This was the signal for an uproar of almost unprecedented proportions in the international strategic community. The Soviet Union, which had itself been conducting research into ballistic missile defence for several years, reacted with predictable expressions of outrage. 'Peace' movements all over the world joined in, never reluctant to accept the intellectual and moral force of any position advanced from Moscow. Even America's allies began the familiar ritual hand-wringing which attends any expression of strength and resolution emanating from Washington.

The latent anti-Americanism which is never far below the surface in certain bands of the political spectrum in Western Europe was brought out for yet another airing. The most bizarre aspect of the hostile reaction to the Strategic Defence Initiative was the closing of ranks around the concept of Mutual Assured Destruction, or MAD. This is the articulation of the form of mutual deterrence sometimes referred to as 'the balance of terror'.

Simply stated, it is the belief that, as long as each side in the nuclear confrontation has enough nuclear weapon systems to absorb a sudden attack by the other, and still retaliate with devastating effect, no one will start a nuclear war. It is a powerful argument; but it rests, obviously, upon the threat to destroy cities and kill millions of innocent citizens; a retaliatory strike, by definition, could not be against the enemy's missiles, since he has already fired them. A corollary to this concept is that neither side should take any steps to protect its citizens against nuclear attack, since this would theoretically enable it to strike first without fear of retaliation. It is, therefore, a deterrent posture based upon the implied readiness to commit collective suicide rather than to surrender; and it has been, until now, regarded as the only sure guarantee of peace between the superpowers and their allies.

This doctrine has provided the basis for the development of the United States nuclear striking force, which has taken the form of a series of improvements in the 'second strike' capacity, that is, in the American ability to absorb a nuclear attack and still inflict unacceptable damage on the cities of the Soviet Union; but a doctrine of this kind has little validity unless both sides subscribe to it. Indeed, the entire MAD theory rests on the assumption that the Soviet Union constructs its strategic doctrines and develops its nuclear weapons in the same way. The fact is that, hitherto, it never has.

Soviet nuclear strategy has in the past been based, not on the assumption that a war might be limited, but on the premise that it will inevitably develop into an extensive exchange of nuclear weapons. In this exchange the Soviets were resolved not only to survive, but to prevail – it was to be a war-fighting and war-winning strategy, not one of simple deterrence. It is true that this strategic concept has recently been called into question by Mr Gorbachev, who told a visiting American group in Moscow in February that the Soviet Union now subscribed to the view that nuclear war is, indeed, unwinnable. The existing Soviet missile armoury was, however, constructed on the 'war-winning' assumption. Russian planners have developed the Soviet offensive missile system to implement their own strategy, rather than the one which advocates of MAD would prefer them to have. In other words, they have created an array of nuclear weapons of great flexibility, designed in certain circumstances to be effective in a first strike.

Fears of this first began to emerge in the late 1970s, when American intelligence sources forecast the appearance of a 'window of vulnerability' in the 1980s. The basis of this assessment was that, while the United States had been failing throughout the 1970s to take the decisions needed to modernize its nuclear weapons systems and protect them from attack, the Soviet Union had been increasing the yield, accuracy and penetrative power of its own ICBMs. Many observers believed that, by the end of the 1970s, a situation had already been reached in which, *whatever the United States might do to remedy the matter*, a period of great danger would begin soon after 1985. The scenario was that, by that time, the Soviet Union would have achieved a nuclear striking force which would be capable, in a first strike, of destroying a large proportion of the American land-based ICBM force in its silos, using only a relatively small proportion of their own missiles. At this stage, if the United States were to retaliate with what was left of its ICBMs, the Soviet Union would have a large enough force left to destroy the entire United States. It would therefore be in a position to impose a system of nuclear blackmail on the West.

It was into this precarious strategic environment that President Reagan launched his Strategic Defence Initiative. The theory which lies behind SDI is that, if it were possible to devise a defensive system capable of destroying a substantial proportion of incoming ballistic missiles (say 50 per cent or more), this would have a significant effect on the nature of deterrence. As a potential aggressor would have no way of knowing *which* five out of every ten missiles launched would fail to reach their target, his options would be limited and his expectations of a successful first strike correspondingly diminished.

The concept of strategic defence on which the principal research effort is being concentrated under the SDI is the 'layered' defence – a system designed to destroy enemy missiles at various stages in their trajectory. The typical trajectory of a ballistic missile consists of four phases. In the *boost phase* (which for an ICBM of the present generation lasts about three minutes) the missile is lifted out of its silo and carried through and out of the atmosphere by its first-, second- and third-stage booster rockets. Each rocket burns for about a minute, propelling the vehicle at an increasing speed to a height of about two hundred kilometres. By the end of this phase, the missile is travelling at about seven kilometres a second. The vehicle then enters the *post-boost phase* which lasts about seven minutes. At this stage, still powered by a low-thrust rocket, it drops off up to ten multiple independently targeted re-entry vehicles – MIRVs – in a programmed sequence and each on its separate trajectory. Along with these, the post-boost vehicle may also deploy with each MIRV a number of decoys and other 'penetration aids'.

The MIRVs and decoys then enter the *mid-course phase*, which is entirely ballistic, that is to say, like a shell fired from a gun, rising to their highest point or *apogee* at a height of about one thousand kilometres before heading back to earth. This phase lasts about twenty minutes, leading to the *terminal phase*, when the MIRVs and decoys re-enter the earth's atmosphere at an altitude of about fifty kilometres. After about one and a half minutes of re-entry, the warheads detonate over their targets. If it were possible to achieve even a 50 per cent destruction rate *in each phase or layer*, a simple mathematical calculation shows that only six or seven warheads out of every hundred launched would reach their target: a 93–94 per cent effective defence.

The technology of intercepting warheads in the terminal phase is reasonably accessible. It relies upon well-researched ballistic-missile defence techniques and envisages largely ground-based or air-launched systems. The crucial problem is the boost phase. The largest Soviet missiles carry at least ten warheads each, and it is therefore essential, if the calculus of the 'layered defence' is to be achieved, to destroy these missiles at the beginning of their flight trajectory, before the warheads can be separated. But this is also the most difficult problem technically – that of destroying a missile deep in enemy territory within seconds of its launch. There are a number of possible techniques. One is the laser, a coherent beam which, travelling at the speed of light, has virtually 'zero time to target'. Its effect is to burn through or melt the metal skin of a missile, causing it to disintegrate. Another technique envisages the use of a neutral particle beam, which involves firing a stream of hydrogen atoms, travelling at about 60,000 miles per second. These pass through the skin of the missile and disrupt its computerized guidance system. It is also theoretically possible to intercept missiles in flight with pellets, or other metal fragments which, on impact, destroy the missile by kinetic energy. One of the technologies capable of achieving this has been described as a kind of Gatling gun capable of firing a million pellets in one second, with a muzzle velocity of 4000 feet per second. These form a cloud of pellets 4000 feet long and hundreds of feet in diameter through which the MIRVs of an offensive missile would have to pass. The tracking and accuracy problems involved in all these technologies are formidable, but, according to American scientists, not insuperable.

The real problem is that, unlike defence systems designed to intercept missiles in mid-course or terminal phases, lasers and neutral particle beams need 'line of sight' basing – that is to say, the generator of the beams must have a direct and unobstructed field of fire at all enemy missile launchers. In other words, they, or mirrors to reflect them, have to be based in space. An effective boost-phase defence therefore needs a fleet of satellites in orbit, ideally large enough to ensure that satellites are over all twenty-two Soviet missile fields at any time, ready to attack all 1400 Soviet land-based ICBMs if, in the worst case, they were launched simultaneously.

An alternative is a 'pop-up' system, which would be deployed only at the time of attack – a solution which would reduce the vulnerability of the defences to counter-attack, but which would, of course, suffer from formidable time constraints. 'Pop-up' interceptors might be launched from submarines cruising in the Arabian or Norwegian seas. An interceptor of this kind would have to rise to about one thousand kilometres before it could 'see' a Soviet ICBM in its boost phase. This technology, of course, depends for its potential effectiveness on the assumption that the Soviet Union will not build ICBMs with a boost phase so short that no 'pop-up' system could 'see' the missile before the booster had burned out.

A ballistic missile defence system would have to perform certain essential functions in each phase of the layered defence. First, it would have to carry out the immensely complicated task of maintaining a constant watch over the entire enemy ICBM force (*surveillance*); and to react immediately to the launch of an offensive missile, and instantly compute its trajectory and probable target (*acquisition*). It must then distinguish in the post-boost phase between a warhead and a decoy (*discrimination*). Next it would have to monitor the exact trajectory of the missile and its warheads at every second of their flight (*pointing and tracking*); and finally direct one of a number of defensive weapons to destroy the missile or its MIRVs (*interception and destruction*). All these activities, as well as accurate assessments of the number of targets destroyed, requiring high-speed data-processing and advanced information technology, would have to be coordinated with infallible accuracy (*battle management*).

One possible conceptual design for a defence system capable of this degree of sophistication begins with satellites in geosynchronous orbit – that is, at a height of approximately 36,000 kilometres, where their orbital velocity keeps them over a constant point on the earth's surface. They would carry out the surveillance role using infra-red sensors capable of detecting an ICBM in flight within seconds of launch, and computers programmed to calculate the general target areas. This information would then be communicated instantly to weapon platforms on satellites in lower earth orbit at about 200 kilometres, and simultaneously to a fleet of mid-course sensor satellites, in orbits from 5000 to 25,000 kilometres. These sensors would monitor the deployment of MIRVs and decoys by any missiles which survived the first- or boost-phase defence layer.

The boost-phase weapon platforms meanwhile would use hyper-velocity guns using electromagnetic energy to fire high-speed projectiles on a collision course with the missiles. The kinetic energy released on impact would destroy the missile before it could complete its ascent. Once the three stages of the booster rocket had burnt out on any surviving missiles, they could no longer be detected by the high-orbit infra-red sensors. At this stage the heat source of the post-boost phase would be picked up by the mid-course sensors, and the missiles would once again be attacked by the hypervelocity guns on the boost-phase satellite platforms.

The mid-course sensors would now begin to employ an increasing range of devices to discriminate between MIRVs and decoys, including radar and optical and infra-red sensors. Once the real warheads had been identified, signals transmitted from the space-based sensors would guide thousands of small ground-based rockets into the path of the MIRVs. As they approached the re-entry vehicles, they would release their own warheads, non-nuclear projectiles which home on to their targets and destroy them on impact.

Finally, information from the mid-course sensors would be 'handed over' to infra-red sensors carried in high-altitude aircraft, launched on warning of attack. These would work in conjunction with radars on the ground to detect any warheads which had escaped the earlier defensive layers, and when the final trajectory had been precisely computed, terminal interceptors would be launched. As it would be necessary to intercept the warheads while they were still high in the atmosphere in order to minimize the effect on the ground of any nuclear explosion, these would be high-acceleration rockets with on-board guidance systems. As soon as they arrived near their targets they would explode a cloud of metal pellets into the paths of the descending warhead, or guide a mini-missile, or 'smart rock', on a collision course, destroying the warhead by kinetic energy. This technique of terminal defence was, incidentally, successfully tested on 10 June 1984, when the US Army intercepted and destroyed an oncoming 'enemy' warhead at a height of 100 miles.

Throughout this short, incredibly complicated engagement, a battle management system would operate, consisting of a network of very fast, high-capacity computers in space and on the ground. Each defensive layer also would have its own battle management system, which would direct the engagement in its own layer, and be connected with the systems of other layers to which it could pass on the results of its own intercepts and the details of surviving missiles. The overall C^3 (command, control and communications) system would provide the link between all the components of all the layers. One of the major problems to be resolved is the question of whether, once such a system had been programmed and deployed, there would be the need, or indeed the time, for human decision-making.

The implications of such a defensive system are clearly far-reaching, and bring into question most of the basic assumptions upon which the East–West confrontation rests, not least in the field of arms control negotiations. The implications fall into two main categories – the relevance of SDI to existing arms control agreements and its possible impact on current and future arms control negotiations. It can be demonstrated with a reasonable degree of certainty that *research* into ballistic missile defence, whether based on the ground, in the atmosphere, or in space, contravenes *no* existing arms control agreement.

The most significant existing agreement in this context is the Anti-Ballistic Missile Treaty of 1972. This treaty forbade the development by the United States and the Soviet Union of ABM systems (including, under Article 21(c), ABM radars) with the exception of one system to defend the capital city and one system to protect its ICBM silos. A protocol to this treaty, signed in 1974, amended this provision to allow only one system on each side – the United States choosing to protect its missile sites and the Soviet Union choosing to defend Moscow. In the event the United States dismantled its own ABM system in the 1970s while the Soviet Union has maintained, and indeed improved, its ballistic missile defences around Moscow.

Beyond this, the treaty specified, in Article 5(1), that each signatory undertook 'not to develop, test, or deploy ABM systems which are sea-based, space-based, or mobile land-based'. The important omission here, of course, is *research*. Those who drafted and negotiated the 1972 treaty recognized that an agreement to abandon research into ballistic missile defence would be impossible to verify. The treaty, under Article 12(1), provided for verification of compliance by 'national technical means' – in other words, there was to be no international or 'on-site' inspection. It would therefore clearly be impossible, even if it were desirable, to arrive at a verifiable agreement on research. The inescapable conclusion is that the Strategic Defence Initiative, so long as it is restricted to research, is not in contravention of the ABM Treaty.

Whatever may be the impact of the Strategic Defence Initiative on current arms control agreements, it is clear that the concept on which the initiative is based implies a totally new approach to arms control in the future. If the research programme should prove that a multi-layered defence system is feasible, using the technologies now under consideration, the United States will then have to decide whether to develop, test and deploy such systems. The dividing line between research and development is not, in general, easy to define. When Ambassador Gerard Smith, the chief American negotiator of the ABM Treaty, testified before the Senate Armed Services Committee in 1972 he interpreted the treaty in these terms:

> The obligation not to develop such systems, devices or warheads would be applicable only to the stage of development which follows laboratory development and testing. The prohibitions on development contained in the ABM Treaty would start at that part of the development process where field testing is initiated on either a prototype or a breadboard model. It was understood by both sides that the prohibition on 'development' applies to activities involved after a component moves from the laboratory development and testing stage, to the field testing stage wherever performed.

In other words, there is no inhibition against laboratory research of any kind, although this interpretation would, evidently, inhibit proto-type and systems testing as well as engineering development. The United States is in any case already committed to consult its allies before taking this step. Furthermore, such development or deploy-ment would, at present, have to be the subject of consultation with the Soviet Union under the terms of the Agreed Interpretation of the ABM Treaty, by which both sides agreed to discuss limitations on any ABM systems based on new technologies.

If, in spite of all this, the USA goes ahead with development and deployment, the implications for a wide range of existing arms control will be substantial. In the first place, it would clearly be inconsistent not only with the ABM Treaty itself, but with the Agreed Interpretation. There is, however, provision in the treaty for either side to withdraw, giving six months' notice, 'if it decides that extraordinary events related to the subject matter of this Treaty have jeopardized its supreme interests'. It would not be too difficult to conceive of a situation in which 'extraordinary events' might be considered, by either side, to have taken place. Indeed, as far back as 1972, immediately after the signature of the treaty, the United States declared unilaterally that 'if an agreement providing for more comprehensive strategic offensive arms limitation were not achieved within five years, US supreme interest would be jeopardized.' It is possible to speculate that the ABM Treaty already has no very great expectation of life.

Development and testing would, however, have a serious effect on other international agreements. The Nuclear Test Ban Treaty of 1963 forbids the testing of nuclear weapons 'in the atmosphere, beyond its limits, including outer space . . .'. As the activation of certain space-based beam weapons, including X-ray lasers, requires an actual nuclear explosion to provide the power source, it is unlikely that such weapons could be developed without tests in space. Furthermore, if such weapons were deployed in space, even without testing, they would contravene the Outer Space Treaty of 1967. It seems clear, therefore, that the strategic concept behind the Strategic Defence Initiative calls for an entirely new approach to the doctrines underlying arms control policies.

It is important at the outset to establish a realistic point of departure. In considering the impact of the SDI on arms control, it should not be assumed that all arms control agreements are necessarily desirable. If an arms control agreement is either unverifiable or unenforceable, it serves Soviet purposes. Arms control should be a facet of defence policy, and agreements which do not enhance security are worse than no agreements at all. In this context President Reagan's Strategic Defence Initiative provides the catalyst for an entirely new approach, in the period between now and the end of the century, to the central political and ideological confrontation – that between the Soviet Union and its allies on the one hand and the United States and its allies on the other.

If the research programme suggests that defence against nuclear missiles might be feasible, it will then be appropriate to move into a new, transitional phase. It can be assumed that the Soviet Union will have continued its own ballistic missile research and development programme; and somewhere around the turn of the century it might prove possible to move to a strategic relationship which will place greater reliance on defence and less on retaliation. At this stage it will be necessary for the United States to take account of the interests and preoccupations of its allies; and also of the implications for international agreements – notably the ABM Treaty with the Soviet Union. It will be important, too, to ensure that any defensive system which it is proposed to deploy suffers from none of the deficiencies now confidently foreshadowed by the opponents of SDI. The defensive systems themselves must be 'survivable', that is to say, not vulnerable to a first strike; otherwise the charge of 'destabilization' would be justified. Furthermore they must not be so expensive that they could easily be outflanked by relatively inexpensive increments to the offensive capability of the other side; in other words, they must be 'cost-effective at the margin'.

During this period, close continuing contacts with the Soviet Union in the field of arms control would be of crucial importance. There would, ideally, be further verifiable reductions in offensive systems. The development and deployment of ballistic missile defences would proceed systematically, and, to a large extent, bilaterally, that is to say, in cooperation with the Soviet Union. Meanwhile the West would have to continue to enhance its conventional defensive capability. At this stage, too, it would also be necessary to begin to engage the other nuclear-weapons powers, as well as the 'near-nuclear-weapons powers', in the process. This phase might well need to be spread over a period of twenty to twenty-five years.

At this stage there is a significant difference of approach, even among those who support the Strategic Defence Initiative. President Reagan, in his original March 1983 speech, spoke of 'rendering these nuclear weapons impotent and obsolete' and of paving the way for 'arms control measures to eliminate the weapons themselves'. The official view of the US administration is that, in the long term, it will be possible to continue, as Paul Nitze has said, 'the reduction of nuclear weapons down to zero'. Others believe that it will always be necessary to retain a residual nuclear capability.

The arguments against the 'abolition' or 'elimination' of nuclear weapons are reasonably familiar. The principal objection is that they cannot be abolished. The knowledge of how to make nuclear weapons cannot be expunged from the collective human consciousness; and there is always the danger, in some international crisis, that one side or the other will decide that sooner than be dictated to, it will construct and use or threaten to use a nuclear weapon. Those who believe that nuclear weapons *can*, eventually, be eliminated claim that, given the deployment of effective non-nuclear defences, cheating by the clandestine construction of nuclear delivery systems would have to be on such a large scale that it would be relatively easy to detect and counteract.

Even if this were true, it would still not deal with the contingency of the terrorist state, and such phenomena as the 'suitcase bomb'. However, even if it proved, in the long term, impossible to eliminate nuclear weapons entirely, there is general agreement among supporters of the Strategic Defence Initiative that nuclear weapons systems could be reduced to a level consistent with 'minimum deterrence', thus removing the instability posed by the potential threat of a first strike. Whether nuclear weapons continued to exist or not, the dangers of nuclear war would have been substantially reduced. This is, of course, a distant vision. It will not be realized, if it is realized at all, until well into the twenty-first century, and it will be formidably expensive. Yet, leaving aside the facile arguments, most of which lack substance, about the need to 'divert military spending into resources to combat starvation in the Third World', few people would dissent from President Reagan's proposition that it is 'worth every investment to free the world from the threat of nuclear war'.

Those who oversimplify the profoundly complicated issue of the Strategic Defence Initiative with objections to 'extending the arms race into space' seem to be prepared to ignore the fact that the confrontation between the superpowers already depends to a large extent upon the military exploration of space. None of the strategic nuclear weapons systems at present deployed could function effectively without the satellites now in orbit to provide early warning, reconnaissance, communications and target information. By the end of 1983, there were at least 2000 military satellites in orbit, engaged in a wide range of military applications.

Space already plays a significant role in contemporary military strategy. It will inevitably continue to do so, since there is no existing international agreement regulating the military uses of space, with the exception of the 1967 Outer Space Treaty forbidding the placing in orbit of weapons of mass destruction. It would therefore be unwise for those involved with the development of military strategy to assume that space may not, before too long, prove to be the 'high ground' which is the traditional concern of the military planner. The Strategic Defence Initiative is too important and too complicated to be assailed with arguments derived from discredited strategic doctrines and based upon traditional habits of strategic thought. Britain, like the rest of Western Europe, is obliged to accept the real possibility that, in the early years of the next century, effective defence against nuclear attack will be a significant element in the deterrent policies of the United States *and* the Soviet Union. This has special implications for the future of the British nuclear striking force.

CHAPTER FIFTEEN

───────◆───────

The British Nuclear Deterrent

The nuclear element of Britain's contribution to the Western Alliance is a striking force consisting, at present, of four Polaris submarines, each capable of striking at targets in the Soviet Union with sixteen long-range missiles equipped with nuclear warheads in the megaton range. Of these four submarines, one is constantly on station and at a high degree of combat readiness. These vessels and their missiles are normally assigned to the Supreme Allied Commander Europe, and their targets are determined by him. In a national emergency, however, it would be possible for the British government unilaterally to resume the sole responsibility both for allocating the targets and firing the missiles.

This force, sometimes described as the 'independent nuclear deterrent', therefore has two distinct politico-military functions. In the first place it contributes to the overall power of the Allied nuclear arsenal, the principal function of which is to deter the Soviet Union from using its conventional forces to attack Western Europe by posing the implicit threat of an early resort by NATO to the use of nuclear weapons. Although it can be argued that the American nuclear capability is so enormous that the relatively small British contribution is numerically irrelevant, this is to ignore the important psychological importance to the Alliance of having a nuclear retaliatory capability outside the direct control of the United States. Its second function is, as a weapon of last resort, to deter the Soviet Union from contemplating a nuclear attack upon the United Kingdom, by posing the threat of instant *British* retaliation against Soviet cities and military installations.

Conventional and nuclear forces, if kept at adequate strength and at an appropriate state of combat readiness, combine to provide an effective deterrent against Soviet attack or nuclear blackmail. Those who now advocate the unilateral renunciation of the nuclear element in this deterrent must therefore submit themselves to the intellectual discipline of constructing an alternative system of national security. At this stage it is appropriate to consider the underlying motives and arguments of the unilateralist school.

It has to be said, at the risk of being accused of witch-hunting, that a small but significant number of those who advocate unilateral disarmament do so because they wish to see this country defenceless against the designs of the Soviet Union. To categorize them as 'communists' or 'Marxists' is not an especially illuminating exercise. They are, however, agents of Soviet influence, whether conscious or unconscious, and they ply their trade in many disguises – as teachers, professors, television producers, civil servants and Members of Parliament. They manipulate and exploit the machinery of democracy with the single aim of destroying it. By exploiting the Campaign for Nuclear Disarmament, they have brought their influence to bear upon a broad constituency ranging, as Sir Michael Howard the historian has put it, 'from saintly men of penetrating intelligence to mindless fanatics impervious to reasoned argument'.

There are, of course, many more people who advocate unilateral nuclear disarmament from a depth of sincere conviction. They believe in the provision of effective arrangements for defence but argue that the British nuclear striking force is at best irrelevant and at worst potentially damaging to national security. The arguments which they deploy usually fall into one or more of three broad categories – moral, political and economic.

The moral argument rests upon the proposition that nuclear weapons are so appallingly and indiscriminately destructive that to use them in war is immoral, because their evil effect would be disproportionate to any good that might theoretically be secured by their use. This belief has impeccable antecedents in the traditional Christian formulation of the doctrine of the just war – specifically in the concepts of proportionality and discrimination. It is possible to argue, of course, that a nuclear weapon is no more immoral than any other weapon used to kill people. It is certainly difficult for a reasonable man to draw any valid moral distinction between nuclear weapons on the one hand and, on the other, chemical or microbiological agents, the high-explosive and incendiary bombs which were used to destroy Coventry, Dresden and Hamburg, or even the artillery shells which helped to reduce the abbey at Monte Cassino to a heap of rubble.

Nevertheless, it would be perverse to reject the proposition that nuclear weapons are different, not merely in scale but in kind, from any other weapons of war, if only because of the potential genetic effects of nuclear radiation; and that, therefore, their *use* as weapons of mass destruction against civilian populations would· be immoral. There remains, however, the question of whether the *threat* of their use as a deterrent is also immoral. The position of some Christians is that the conditional intent in this case is no different from the action – that a threat to carry out an immoral act is as immoral as the act itself. This point of view seems to take insufficient account of another important element in the doctrine of the just war – that concerning the justice of the aim.

To use a simple everyday analogy, there would seem to be a valid moral distinction between the behaviour of a man who threatens violence in defence of his own person or property and that of the man who does so in the commission of robbery or rape. Similarly, in the doctrine of the just war, as Julian Lider has pointed out in his book *On the Nature of War*, the justification most widely accepted through-out history (and in all belief systems) has been defence against aggression. The strategy of the Western Alliance involves the threat of nuclear retaliation to deter a potential enemy from attacking the West, either with his own nuclear weapons or with his demonstrably superior conventional forces. The Soviet doctrine envisages that nuclear wea-pons might be used in *any* military conflict, including one in which their use became necessary to overcome the enemy's defences. In this context the moral objection to the possession of nuclear weapons as a deterrent seems to be less persuasive.

The political or strategic arguments for unilateral disarmament by the United Kingdom rest upon the proposition that the possession of nuclear weapons is intrinsically provocative, and that if Britain were to abandon them we would cease to be a target for nuclear attack. This ignores the inconvenient historical fact that on the only occasion on which nuclear weapons have been used in war, they were used against a country which had no capacity to retaliate. In any case, in the British context it is an obscure argument, since the British strategic nuclear striking force is submarine-based. It would therefore be left intact by a pre-emptive strike directed at the territory of the United Kingdom. The cosy assumption that unilateral disarmament would in itself provide us with a nuclear sanctuary has very little basis in reality.

The economic arguments are even less convincing. The standard references to the 'crippling cost of nuclear weapons', with the corollary, spoken or implicit, that they are taking bread out of the mouths of the poor, are not easy to reconcile with the fact that the cost of maintaining the Polaris force is £126 million a year – that is to say, one fifth of one per cent of the gross national product; or, to put it another way, substantially less than the annual budget of the London Borough of Camden. Much of the public misapprehension about the cost of nuclear weapons springs from the published estimates of the capital cost of a new generation of nuclear missiles – the Trident system – with which the government proposes to replace Polaris.

It is this issue which has been the catalyst for the latest phase in the public debate about Britain's defence policy. The Labour Party has incorporated into its proposals for the defence of the United Kingdom the principal elements of unilateralism – the 'decommissioning' of the present Polaris missile force; the cancellation of the Trident programme; and the removal of all American nuclear weapons and nuclear bases from British soil. The Alliance of the Liberal and Social Democratic parties accepts the need for a British nuclear striking force, but suspects that Trident is the wrong way to provide it. They propose, if they should have a voice at all in deciding upon this matter, to examine the possibility of other delivery systems. The Trident programme is therefore at the heart of the argument about a future defence policy for this country.

In these circumstances it is incumbent on everyone who thinks about strategy and defence policy seriously to make a rational assessment of the underlying assumptions implicit in Britain's nuclear strategy. As a point of departure, it is necessary to answer two basic questions. The first is – does the United Kingdom still need a nuclear striking force of its own? If the answer is yes, what sort of weapon system does it need?

No one attempting to answer the question of whether Britain needs a nuclear striking force can ignore the fact that *it already has one*. In sheer practical terms, the process of 'giving it up' poses problems which have never been sufficiently addressed, such as the safe disposal of the weapons and warheads already in existence. It is true that these difficulties are not insuperable; they indicate, however, that nothing to do with nuclear strategy is ever entirely simple or straightforward.

A more substantial argument about giving up the military capacity to deliver nuclear weapons already in our possession concerns the whole context of international negotiations, especially in the field of arms control. It would surely be irresponsible to renounce such a capability without obtaining some major concession in return. This would, of course, have to be a concession from the Soviet Union which had a substantial effect on the overall East–West balance, not some derisory arrangement whereby in exchange for the abandonment by Britain of all its 64 ballistic missiles, the Soviet Union agreed to reduce its own stockpile of ICBM launchers from 1398 to 1334 – a suggestion which had a brief moment of glory after the visit of a group of Labour politicians to Moscow in 1986.

In any case, the abandonment of nuclear weapons is not an option which can be considered in a political vacuum. The British nuclear striking force is not *only* an independent nuclear deterrent usable in the last resort to threaten a potential attacker in the absence of a nuclear guarantee from any other power. It is an integral part of the whole complex of NATO strategy.

At the most obvious level, as Mr Denis Healey used to argue, it provides a second centre of decision-making which presents the leaders of the Soviet Union with an added complication in their strategic

ions. To put the matter at its crudest, if Soviet military plan-
templated an action of some kind in Western Europe which
:ved would not cause the United States to threaten the use of
нии nuclear striking forces, they could not be sure, however remote
the possibility might seem to academic strategists, that the British
government would not threaten the use of its own nuclear striking
force either in isolation, or possibly in collaboration with the third
centre of decision-making – France.

This line of argument sometimes leads to what is known as the
'catalytic' theory of nuclear deterrence which, put in its simplest form,
envisages that if a situation arose in which the European nuclear powers
believed that vital national or regional interests were at stake, but in
which the United States was reluctant to use the threat of its own
nuclear weapons, the threat or the use of French or British nuclear
weapons would have the catalytic effect of forcing the United States
into the equation. This is not a contingency which is, in reality, likely
to arise, but it indicates the extent to which British nuclear weapons
are already tightly woven into the whole fabric of Western defence and
deterrence.

Finally, there is the argument that the United States feels under-
standably reluctant to carry the whole burden of moral responsibility
for deterring the Soviet Union from military attack by the threat of
nuclear weapons and wishes to count on the support of at least one of
its allies. The French, of course, are not members of the integrated
military structure of NATO; Britain therefore provides the United
States with its only close support in the nuclear confrontation.

To these considerations of the collective security of the Western
Alliance must be added the not inconsiderable possibility that Britain's
nuclear striking force might pose an independent deterrent against an
attack upon this country or its vital interests. It has been fashionable
over the years, and at some stages in the development of nuclear
strategy even valid, to suggest that there are *no* circumstances in which
the United Kingdom might credibly threaten to use its own nuclear
weapons if the United States were not prepared to threaten the use of
theirs. Although this may have been true at certain stages in the de-

velopment of nuclear strategy, it is now an extremely dubious proposition.

In the first place, it is by no means out of the question that there might arise in the not too distant future a situation in which, either through the further development of space-based defence systems or through bilateral arms control agreements of the kind now under discussion, there might be some kind of 'stand-off' between the superpowers – namely, a situation in which the use of nuclear weapons by either of them against the other had become demonstrably ineffective and therefore incredible as a threat. Premonitions of this emerged at the meeting between Mr Reagan and Mr Gorbachev at Reykjavik in 1986 when there were on the table, if only for a short time, proposals that the United States and the Soviet Union should give up all ballistic nuclear missiles and withdraw from Europe all intermediate-range nuclear weapons. The second of these proposals is now the subject of serious consideration by the superpowers.

There might be a temptation on the part of Soviet planners to calculate that they could then use conventional forces to attain limited objectives in Western Europe – and even conceivably in the United Kingdom – without the danger of intervention by the United States. However dogmatically Western theorists might dismiss the possibility that a British government would threaten to use, much less actually use, nuclear weapons in these circumstances, no responsible or sane Soviet planner would be likely to base his calculations on such an uncertain assumption.

Furthermore, it must now be accepted that the strategy of nuclear non-proliferation has, for all practical purposes, failed. For some time only five powers – the five permanent members of the United Nations Security Council, namely the United States, the Soviet Union, France, Britain and China – possessed nuclear weapons. The only obvious and clear nuclear threat to the West has been posed by the Soviet Union. For various reasons, some of which have already been examined, the People's Republic of China has not posed and still does not pose a military threat to the West.

More recently, however, it has become clear that several other countries now have the capacity to produce and stockpile nuclear weapons and to construct effective, if limited, delivery systems. Indeed, there is very strong evidence that a number of countries, such as India, Israel and South Africa, already have a nuclear weapons capability either laboratory-tested or, in the case of South Africa and India, possibly fully tested. Countries such as Pakistan, Japan and Argentina undoubtedly have the scientific and industrial base to construct a modest nuclear striking force if they should believe it in their national interest to do so. Furthermore, even if this were not sufficiently de-stabilizing, there is strong evidence that Middle Eastern countries such as Iraq and Libya have been making strenuous attempts over a number of years to acquire nuclear weapons of their own. In these circum-stances, the abandonment by Britain of its own nuclear capability is no simple matter.

It has to be considered not only in the context of the major East–West confrontation, but also in the context of a world in which the spread of nuclear weapons becomes more and more likely as the technology of their manufacture becomes simpler and more widely known. There is, therefore, a strong presumption that unless more powerful arguments can be deployed for the abandonment of the existing British nuclear weapons capacity, and unless some clear advantage in the field of international relations and arms control negotiations could be obtained in exchange, Britain should certainly retain a capacity for nuclear deterrence.

There is, in any case, a more powerful and subtle argument against any proposal for unilateral nuclear disarmament. The two principal arguments deployed by those who wish to abandon Britain's nuclear capacity are the practical matter of cost and the more sophisticated case of the moral imperative. The cost argument can be dealt with fairly simply. In the first place, the running costs of our existing nuclear striking force are minimal. They represent only a very small percentage of our total defence budget, and the saving from decommissioning the current Polaris fleet would be marginal. The capital cost of replacing Polaris is, of course, much more substantial. However, even taking the worst financial case, the possible cost of the replacement now envisaged

– the Trident system – is not as ruinous as it has been represented to be, especially if it is amortized over the years of the development and deployment of the system.

The arguments of the unilateralists about the effect of the savings if this system were cancelled do not really stand up to close examination. The more extreme prudential argument of the 'peace people' is that this money should be devoted instead to good works, such as the relief of famine in the Third World and a redistribution of global resources. Anyone who has studied the matter with any degree of political objectivity knows that the transfer of resources which this implies is no simple matter; in any case it can be fairly clearly demonstrated that even if the entire sum saved from Trident were devoted to aid to the Third World, the impact on development problems would be insignificant.

The less extreme position is the one at present adopted by the leadership of the Labour Party – namely that the savings from the adoption of a non-nuclear defence policy would be devoted to improving our conventional defences. It can be fairly clearly demonstrated, however, that the increment to our land forces, air forces, surface or submarine fleets which would be made possible by cancellation of Trident would be no more than marginal and would certainly not enable us to pose, in the face of the current Russian threat, a *conventional* deterrent. The addition of an armoured division in Germany, or a few frigates or fighter aircraft to the navy or the air force is unlikely to provide for Russian planners the same problems as those which they have to contemplate when confronted with a modern and effective nuclear strike force.

Finally, it is necessary to consider the effect on the Atlantic Alliance of a decision by Britain to abandon its nuclear capability. In this context the moral dimension has to be considered. The proposition that we should give up our nuclear striking force because the use of nuclear weapons is immoral, and because the threat of their use is equally immoral, requires much closer examination. In the first place, even if the use of nuclear weapons is seen to be immoral – a complicated argument in itself – it is by no means as clear that the *threat* of their use is equally immoral. Many distinguished churchmen argue that the use of force of any kind can be morally distinguished from the *conditional intent* to use it. This is, however, a profound moral and ethical argument about which even distinguished theologians differ.

Nevertheless, anyone who holds the view that we should abandon our own nuclear striking force because its use *or the threat of its use* is immoral must surely regard it as equally immoral to rely on a nuclear guarantee from any other country. In that case, two consequences would follow. The first is that we could not allow the United States to use any installation in this country as a base from which to deliver its own nuclear weapons. This is the conclusion which the Labour Party has apparently drawn. Such a conclusion, however, carries with it a further and even more serious corollary.

If it is accepted that we cannot rely upon the use or threat of the use of nuclear force because it is intrinsically immoral, then, quite clearly, it would be entirely illogical to continue to be a member of the North Atlantic Treaty Organization since its entire strategy is based upon the ultimate threat of nuclear retaliation. The logical consequence, therefore, of a decision to adopt a 'non-nuclear' strategy is withdrawal from NATO and the adoption of a foreign policy of neutrality or non-alignment. To pretend otherwise is profoundly dishonest. The Labour Party leadership has not, so far, accepted this logic – arguing that, like Norway or Luxembourg, Britain can remain an effective member of NATO without nuclear weapons or nuclear bases. While this might satisfy a country aspiring to no greater influence in the world than that of Norway or Luxembourg, it is unlikely to appeal to those who believe that Britain should not be content to play a tame or minor role in the affairs of the free world. Meanwhile a substantial element in the Labour Party *is* prepared to accept the logic of unilateralism and to disengage from the Western Alliance. It is an element which would have an influential voice if the Labour Party under its present leadership ever succeeded in forming a government.

In any case, it is extremely unlikely that the United States would be prepared to contemplate a situation in which its major ally renounced its nuclear weapons and removed American bases from British territory while the American government and people continued to bear the cost and moral responsibility of defending the very country which had implemented these policies. The inevitable result of a policy of unilateral nuclear disarmament by this country would be, therefore, to weaken and eventually to unravel the North Atlantic Treaty Organization and to accelerate the American tendency to withdraw into Fortress America, abandoning the entangling Alliance which is already of dubious value in the eyes of many Americans; and which, in the event of unilateral nuclear disarmament by Britain, would be seen as an almost unlimited liability.

If, then, it seems sensible to conclude that Britain needs a nuclear striking force, not only now but in the future, it is then necessary to decide what kind of system it should be. Most observers agree that the present Polaris system, although effective for the moment, will not continue to be so for much longer. In passing, it might be said that the present force is only *just* adequate, in that with four boats in commission we can only guarantee to have one on station at any given time. Given the improvements in anti-submarine warfare which are likely to take place in the coming years, it is doubtful that we should continue to rely for very much longer on a marginal capacity of that kind.

With one boat on station carrying sixteen missiles equipped with the improved Chevaline warheads, there is still sufficient potential penetrative and destructive power to cause doubts in the mind of any Soviet planner. However, faced with a constant improvement in anti-submarine warfare, a credible deterrent needs to have greater range – not necessarily to strike at more distant targets from present operational areas, but primarily to provide greater flexibility in the extent of the operational areas themselves. Furthermore the current Polaris system, even with the Chevaline warheads, is unlikely to be able to penetrate an enhancement of the present ABM system deployed around Moscow, much less the sophisticated, possibly space-based, strategic defence systems of the future. And here it might be relevant to refer briefly to the Soviet strategic defence programme.

So much has been said and written about the American Strategic Defence Initiative that there has been a tendency to ignore the work which the Soviet Union is doing in this field. For many years the Soviet Union has been conducting advanced research in the field of lasers, directed-energy weapons and kinetic-energy weapons. Although the United States is undoubtedly well ahead in some aspects of space-based defence research and certainly has the potential to widen the gap between it and the Soviet Union, there is little doubt that in some areas the Soviet Union itself is well advanced. Furthermore the phased array radar system at Krasnoyarsk, in spite of persistent Soviet denials, is certainly more consistent with the kind of radar system that would be needed for an advanced space-based system than for any of the anti-ballistic missile systems permitted under the current ABM Treaty between the Soviet Union and the United States.

Some of the best scientific and technical minds in the Soviet Union are currently engaged in the research and development of strategic defence systems; and the intensive Soviet campaign against the American Strategic Defence Initiative almost certainly arises from a fear that the scientific and economic resources of the United States would enable the Americans to overtake the Russian effort and to deploy effective strategic defence systems long before the Soviet Union could do so.

It would be prudent for all Western planners, including those who advise the British government, to take account of the possibility that early in the next century the Soviet Union will be in a position to deploy advanced anti-ballistic missile systems including space-based defences. These will probably be capable not only of destroying a proportion of land-based ballistic missiles from the boost phase through the mid-course to the re-entry phase, but also of destroying submarine-launched missiles in the mid-course and re-entry phases, and possibly even of destroying cruise missiles by using some of the techniques which are already emerging from strategic defence research.

When, therefore, an earlier British government came to consider the replacement of Polaris, it had all these factors to take into account – the range and penetrability of the existing missiles, the continued reliability and serviceability of the boats, and the inevitable improvement in Soviet techniques of anti-submarine warfare and defence against ballistic and air-breathing delivery systems. There is, in addition, a consideration which is too often ignored – the importance of having, wherever possible, a common nuclear weapons system with our major ally the United States. This has been at the heart of the development of all our deterrent systems from bombers through the abortive Skybolt system to Polaris, Poseidon, the Trident C4 and now the current plan for the Trident D5.

The Trident C4 was in fact quite well suited to the military require-ments of the United Kingdom. The missile had a range of over 4000 miles, thus increasing the operational range of the submarines. Each missile could deliver up to eight warheads, in the form of multiple independently guided re-entry vehicles, each of which could be directed on to a separate target with an accuracy of about 500 yards. The extra range of the C4 made it unlikely to become vulnerable to foreseeable improvements in Soviet anti-submarine warfare, and the fact that each submarine could carry up to 128 warheads meant that even one boat on station would have the capacity to penetrate present and foreseeable Soviet defences.

The D5, of course, is a very different matter. Each missile will be armed with up to fourteen warheads with an accuracy even greater than that of the C4. It is, indeed, often argued that the D5 is a system of greater accuracy and sophistication than Britain really needs and that it constitutes a provocation to the Soviet Union. Yet, clearly, it would not have made very much sense for the United Kingdom to go ahead with its plans to acquire the C4 system after the United States had decided to move to the D5. Indeed, it is unlikely that the C4 option would even have remained available.

There are, in addition, other arguments in favour of the D5 system. One is flexibility in the arms control process. As Admiral of the Fleet Lord Lewin, a former Chief of the Defence Staff, has pointed out, it would be possible in certain circumstances to put twelve missiles instead of sixteen in the submarine and leave four tubes empty. Similarly it would be possible to vary the warhead content in each missile. All these variations would be available in the context of any future arms control agreement, and some would be clearly verifiable by the Soviet Union using its own national means of surveillance.

The principal argument in favour of the Trident D5, however, is in the context of its effectiveness against future Soviet strategic defences, especially those around Moscow. In analysing Britain's requirement for a future nuclear striking force, it is important to bear one basic factor in mind. Britain does not need, even if it could achieve it, what is known as a 'first-strike capability', in other words a nuclear striking force capable of attacking and destroying Soviet offensive missiles. It needs only a *second-strike* capability, that is, the ability to pose the threat of unacceptable devastation to the Soviet Union in the case of a Soviet attack. This means a counter-city capability rather than a counter-force capability – that is to say, the requirement is to pose a threat to the Soviet population, centres of government and economic production of a kind which would make any Russian attack an unacceptable risk.

This postulates the sombre but inescapable need to be able to strike at the main centre of Soviet government, military command and national administration – in other words, Moscow. Now, the Soviet Union already has, under the terms of the existing ABM Treaty with the United States of America, a ballistic missile defence system deployed to protect its capital city. The Russians are constantly upgrading and enhancing this system and it is already at a stage in development which would give it a considerable defensive capability against the current Polaris system. If the Soviet Union continues to improve its ballistic missile defences around Moscow, and, furthermore, if it develops a strategic defence system depending partly upon space-based systems, it might be possible to achieve a defensive system which would be guaranteed to destroy more than 90 per cent of an incoming ballistic missile attack.

In the case of Polaris, even with a Chevaline warhead, this would be a significant attrition rate; but with the D5 Trident system, on the assumption that we shall still have four boats, the British nuclear striking force would be theoretically capable of delivering 896 multiple independently guided re-entry vehicles at selected Soviet targets.

Therefore, even if the Soviet Union were capable of knocking out 90 per cent of this missile force, there would still be approximately 90 warheads guaranteed to reach their target. As Britain needs only to ensure a second-strike rather than a first-strike capability it would not be important *which* target was reached, as each would be a centre of command, population or economic production.

Even if there were only one boat on station, it would still be able to deliver 224 MIRVed missiles of which, even against the most effective of Soviet strategic defences, more than twenty missiles would still arrive at their targets. If, therefore, the United Kingdom is to have a strategic nuclear striking force which is capable of posing a credible second-strike threat to the Soviet Union, it will be necessary, in the context of the probable anti-submarine warfare and strategic defence techniques of the early years of the next century, to have a system with capabilities very similar to those of the Trident D5.

A number of alternatives for a Polaris replacement have been put forward from time to time, most notably by the Social Democratic and Liberal Alliance. The possibility most frequently canvassed is a cruise missile which would be capable of being fired from a mobile platform such as a submarine. Although it is by no means certain that this would be very much cheaper than a Trident missile, it would, according to those who support the idea, release us from our dependence on the United States in that the missile could be manufactured in the United Kingdom. It is also suggested that this would be less provocative to the Soviet Union while being equally capable of reaching its target.

While these arguments might be valid in the context of the current state of Soviet defences, it is doubtful whether a cruise missile would pose a credible second-strike threat to the Soviet Union in the context of the kind of missile defence systems which will exist in the next century. In any case, the cruise missile, although it might for some time be invulnerable to the kind of techniques being developed for the destruction of ballistic missiles, is, by the very nature of an air-breathing delivery system, relatively slow and therefore vulnerable to less sophisticated defensive systems.

Various other proposals have been put forward, including the possibility of collaboration with the French, the main effect of which, according to those who propose it, would be to reduce the United Kingdom requirement to three boats, and possibly make available the French M4 missile in place of the Trident, thereby reducing our reliance on the United States. All previous attempts at multinational nuclear collaboration have demonstrated, however, that the command and control problems are extremely difficult to overcome. Furthermore, much of Britain's current nuclear weapons capability relies upon technology acquired from the United States of America, of a kind which it would not be possible to share in the context of an Anglo-French agreement. Collaboration with France in the field of nuclear weapons, targeting and strategy is likely to become an important element in future British defence policy. It should not, however, be regarded as an alternative to Trident, but as a catalyst for effective defence co-operation in Western Europe.

CHAPTER SIXTEEN

Mass Communications and National Policy

In a free society arrangements for national security, like most other aspects of national policy, depend upon a high degree of consensus. If the people are to agree to the appropriation of a substantial proportion of national resources for the purpose of maintaining and equipping an effective military establishment, they need to be fully and reliably informed about the nature of any threat which might be posed to their safety and that of their free political institutions. In this process a free press plays a central role.

One of the best loved stories of the Second World War tells of an army General in uniform walking along Whitehall on the way to his club for lunch. He was approached by a civilian who asked politely, 'I wonder if you could tell me which side the Foreign Office is on?' The officer, scarcely pausing in his stride, responded severely, 'Ours, I hope.' It is a sentiment which might nowadays be expressed about the British press, and especially the electronic media, who often seem to take a somewhat perverse and idiosyncratic view of national security in its broader sense – the sense of the safety, stability and quality of life of society. It can be taken as axiomatic that most people of goodwill have a common interest in that kind of security, and that they would regard as hostile and menacing anyone who sought to damage or destroy it – including the media of communication.

Yet some organs of communication decline to accept any responsibility or loyalty higher than that which is summed up by such sentiments as 'the public has a right to know' and 'our only business is to publish the news'. It is therefore important to consider the functions of the media of communication in the defence of a free society. It is unnecessary to consider societies which are not free, since newspapers and broadcasting organizations in such countries are simply instruments of state power.

The first thing to be said is that, within certain limits, the media of communication should be free to examine the activities and behaviour of public institutions and public individuals. Responsible investigative journalism is a necessary safeguard against the kind of corruption and malpractice which can poison the system of liberal democracy. There are, however, certain limits. One concerns the right of individuals – including those in public life – to a degree of privacy and freedom from harassment. The other concerns the moral obligation which a journalist has to contribute to the preservation of the political institutions which guarantee basic freedoms – including the freedom of the press. External and internal security are essential safeguards. This obligation was clearly recognized by Sir Ian Trethowan, when, as Director-General of the BBC, he was replying to criticisms that the Corporation was allowing deliberate denigration of the police. He wrote:

> No broadcaster or, for that matter, newspaperman, will lightly report allegations against the police. We all know that our own freedom and independence rest on parliamentary democracy and the rule of law. But we also know that the enforcement of the law is a matter of legitimate public concern and that freedom must be exercised, albeit with care and responsibility, if it is not to invite erosion.

At first glance that seems to be an unexceptionable statement of the responsibilities of serious journalism; but in introducing his general statement of principle, Sir Ian advanced a proposition which requires a little closer inspection. 'No broadcaster', he writes, 'or, for that matter, newspaperman, will lightly report allegations against the police.'

If that is meant, as it seems, to be a statement of fact, it is one of doubtful validity. In the present climate of society and communications, there is no shortage of broadcasters, and not a few newspapermen, who will not only lightly report allegations against the police, but who are prepared to place disproportionate emphasis on these allegations. The television and radio reporting of the riots outside the Wapping newspaper building in 1987 carried with it very heavy overtones of hostility to the police; and more recently the news of the shooting of an armed man in central London was reported in a way which subtly but unmistakably hinted at the excessive use of force by the police – and this even before the full circumstances were clearly established.

There is, therefore, often a difference between the way in which distinguished practitioners in the media believe they should behave (and, according to Sir Ian Trethowan, think they do behave) and what actually happens in real life. This is, of course, not simply an argument about attitudes to the police. It covers a wide range of issues in which bad communications can distort and corrupt – civil violence, international terrorism, war and the threat of war, secret intelligence and a wide spectrum of military activities.

It would be foolish to attempt to deny that there is widespread concern and anxiety about the way in which the media handle some of these issues. Different considerations and criteria have to be applied to the two principal forms of media: print journalism and the electronic or mass media – sound broadcasting and television. There are a number of reasons for this.

The first is that, in this country as in most liberal democracies, there is a great variety of newspapers and journals from which readers can exercise a choice, with some degree of certainty about the opinions, prejudices and enthusiasms of those who edit and write in the paper concerned. No one takes the *Guardian* expecting to read enthusiastic profiles of Mrs Thatcher or the *Daily Telegraph* for articles endorsing the activities of Monsignor Bruce Kent. Most people therefore tend to read the newspapers which reflect their own views and reinforce their own prejudices; and those who require a broad spectrum of views, news and opinions have access to them if they are prepared to submit to the somewhat harsh discipline of reading several newspapers every day and a few serious magazines every week.

This is not so in the mass media. Broadcasting and television are not quite a monopoly, but it can be seriously claimed that they are, at present, a duopoly. With the development of such techniques as cable TV and direct broadcasting by satellite, this situation may change. It would be foolish indeed to allow these new systems of communication to be appropriated by the existing duopoly. As things stand, however, two broadcasting organizations control the total output of mass communications. There are, theoretically, clear prescriptions and expectations about the degree of objectivity and impartiality which are to be observed by these organizations in their programming – specifically in the field of news and current affairs. Broadcasting – especially on television – therefore imposes limitations, responsibilities and inhibitions which are not present in print journalism.

This is not to say that newspapermen are not under an obligation to be fair, accurate and, indeed, something more than accurate, *truthful* – in their reporting.

There are, however, essential differences between written and electronic communications. Apart from the problems of choice and monopoly, fundamental attributes distinguish television from the other media. Television is, of course, a mass medium. Whereas newspapers and magazines are the principal source of information for the literate, and whereas serious or 'quality' publications count their readers in thousands, television reaches millions – literate and illiterate, sophisticated and simple, educated and ignorant. Furthermore television, by definition, deals predominantly in images. The pictures are the principal vehicle of communication – the words are peripheral or at least secondary.

Practitioners of the world of television understand this well, and a story or a programme has much more chance of being given prominence if the pictures are dramatic. As a result, more time is devoted to visually exciting material – often connected inevitably with violence – than to stories or subjects which might be more significant in the broader context, but which are not so susceptible to visual presentation. The consequence of this is that many people take the view that television is essentially an extension of show-business rather than a medium of communication. Even without taking that extreme view, it is possible to suggest that television is an unsuitable medium for the communication of ideas – especially if those ideas are complicated or sophisticated.

Yet it is self-evident that for the great majority of people, television is the principal, and for some the only, source of news, views and opinions. It formulates their tastes, habits, prejudices and political opinions; and it tends to formulate them instantly – in real time. It is, beyond doubt, the most potent and significant medium of communication in existence and is likely to remain so as far ahead as we can see. For that reason it is appropriate to concentrate on the role which television plays in the broader context of national and international security.

It is arguable that television journalism is an especially acute example of a modern tendency which has been described as 'adversary journalism' – a concept of journalism in which all existing institutions and authorities are regarded as alien, hostile and threatening. It has, to a very large extent, taken the place of really serious journalism, even in some of our 'quality' national newspapers. In television it is rampant. The distinguishing characteristic of serious journalism of the traditional kind was that it examined political and social problems almost from the point of view of an alternative government – as though searching for the measures and solutions for which the journalist himself, might, in other circumstances, be responsible.

Adversary journalism, on the other hand, is instinctively destructive; its purpose is to criticize, oppose and attack existing institutions and conventional standards. This is especially true of television, since the *status quo* is of no visual interest. In normal circumstances the streets of Brixton or Liverpool are not very much different from any other urban environment; one university or polytechnic is very much like another; the streets of Rome or the airport at Vienna are not normally subjects of any great interest. To make them interesting there have to be riots, protest, agitation or violence. Thus there has emerged a kind of empathy between television and violence; and it is not too big a step from there to the situation in which the camera is used to provoke and stimulate the very scenes which turn a commonplace street or a boring airport into a focus of drama and excitement.

The relationship between television and international terrorism has been examined in Chapter 6. It is not only in the context of terrorism, however, that mass communications have a significant impact on national policy. They influence also national perceptions of security and defence policy in their broadest sense. It can be argued, and indeed often is, that American television coverage of the war in Vietnam had a significant impact on the outcome of the war, which has left a lasting scar on the American psyche and profoundly influenced the conduct of American foreign policy. In this context it is interesting to note that there have been no such pressures on Soviet foreign policy in south-west Asia. There are no television crews in Afghanistan.

Television coverage of the British campaign in the Falkland Islands was less traumatic than that of the American war in Vietnam partly because it was, to the fury of many media people, kept more firmly under control. Even so, there was at least one well-authenticated occasion on which media coverage of a projected operation placed the lives of British troops at risk. Indeed, senior military officers go as far as to say that casualties were actually caused by the irresponsibility of a small minority of reporters.

A similar example of sheer stupidity failed only by the merest chance to jeopardize the operation mounted by the SAS against the Iranian embassy terrorists in London in 1980; and, whatever might be regarded as the verdict in the clash between Mr Norman Tebbit and Mr Alasdair Milne, most objective observers would agree that the BBC's coverage of the American bombing of Tripoli and Benghazi left something to be desired in the way of objectivity, impartiality and responsibility.

It is, indeed, in the field of foreign affairs, or international relations, that the media show themselves in their most unattractive and destructive light. When it comes to reporting from distant countries, the left makes the running, which means that the most virulent anti-Americanism has become the norm. We are bombarded with reports about El Salvador and Nicaragua because they can be made the vehicle for stories of American duplicity – real or alleged. There are few reports from African or Asian countries, with Soviet connections, where cruelty and repression are endemic. The whole question of the quality, standards and integrity of foreign reporting in the media needs urgent attention. Foreign news reporting needs to be full, accurate and objective. The selective emphasis of politically motivated presenters and reporters often falls little short of propaganda.

It was the late Sir Huw Wheldon, whose integrity and professionalism were unassailable, who pointed out that the concept of 'balance' in media reporting is sometimes assumed to mean a naive and oversimplified requirement to present the two sides to every question. It is really, as he insisted, more a matter of truth than balance – 'an intelligent effort to make sense of all the facts, however difficult, and not just some of them'.

One of the more subtle means of circumventing these requirements is by the tendentious and inaccurate use of words and phrases. Presenters and reporters often assert that a soldier has been 'interrogated' and 'executed' by Irish terrorists, when they really mean tortured and murdered. The organizations which advocate unilateral disarmament are described as the Peace Movement. Terrorists of certain political persuasions are referred to as 'freedom fighters' or 'urban guerrillas'. Part of this, of course, is insidious brain-washing; and part of it is symptomatic of the appalling decline in the standards of grammar, language and literacy which has taken place in the media over the last twenty-five years.

Much of what is criticized about television journalism is only partly to do with whether it is biased either to the left or the right. Indeed, accusations of that kind come from both ends of the political spectrum, enabling the television authorities to defend themselves with the superficially plausible claim that, if they are attacked from both sides, they must be doing something right. It is, of course, equally logical to conclude that they are doing everything wrong; but this is not the point at issue. The real and relevant charge is that some sections of the media do not seem to have absorbed the fundamental principle that our freedom and independence rest on parliamentary democracy and the rule of law.

There seems to be an instinctive tendency, when faced with a conflict between parliamentary democracy and the rule of law on the one hand and extra-parliamentary activity, lawlessness and violence on the other, to adopt at best a position between the two sides and, at worst, to give the benefit of the doubt to protest movements, radical activists and disaffected minorities. Those who seek in this way some fallacious moral symmetry should remember the words of Sir William Haley, a former editor of *The Times* and Director-General of the BBC: 'Some things are evil, cruel and ugly and no amount of fine writing will make them good or kind or beautiful.' Nor, I would add, any number of dramatic television documentaries.

It has been suggested that there is a need for an organization somewhat similar to the Bar Council or the Law Society to govern and control the activities of practitioners in the mass media. This idea, of course, is not likely to have immediate appeal for those who work in the mass media; indeed, no less eminent a practitioner than Sir Robin Day has already expressed his reservations about it.

It is time, nevertheless, that the role of the media of communications in modern society became a subject of serious debate in this country. So far, the concept of 'adversary journalism' has spilled over into the unseemly brawl which at present passes for public debate. Intemperate attacks on the media lead to equally intemperate replies; when faced with reasonable doubts advanced as a result of serious research, the hierarchy of the BBC and Independent Television tend to dismiss the observations of outsiders as irrelevant, ill-informed or ill-intentioned.

What is at issue is the role of the communications media in the preservation of a free society; and here there is a very delicate balance to be maintained. Even in free societies – *especially* in free societies – most governments would prefer a press that was not too critical or inquisitive. When the media become too importunate even the most tolerant and flexible government begins to look for ways of preventing them from standing in the way of policies which that particular government believes to be desirable; and when the media behave stupidly or irresponsibly in matters affecting official secrets or national security the government's desire for regulatory controls attracts increasing popular support.

At the end of *that* road lies state control and censorship of the press –

a major step in the erosion of liberty; but if it is to be avoided, the media must recognize that while they need hold no loyalty to any government, they *do* have a clear responsibility to society. Part of that responsibility lies in a readiness to defend, endorse and propagate the values of liberal democracy. This includes a constant regard for the instruments and institutions which are necessary to preserve the security of the democratic system. Editors, presenters, writers and all the other practitioners in the media are right to be sensitive to any threat of outside control of their activities; but they should never forget that if, as a result of their activities, our political institutions are weakened, and our defences undermined, and as a result democracy perishes, their concern for editorial independence will be a matter of no more than academic interest.

CHAPTER SEVENTEEN

—◆—

Arms Control and Security

It is impossible to conduct any serious debate on defence policy outside the context of international negotiations on arms control and disarmament. It is possible, of course, that there might emerge, in the next fifteen years or so, international agreements in the field of arms control which might materially change the strategic context. Until this happens, however, it would clearly be irresponsible for any British government unilaterally to abandon its nuclear weapons capability. The weight of logic and evidence suggests that previous governments have made the correct decision in choosing the Trident D5 system as the successor to Polaris. It provides a basis of common procurement with the United States of America; it provides a credible nuclear striking force with sufficient range, throw weight and penetrative power to guarantee to threaten unacceptable damage on the centres of Soviet government even in the context of ballistic missile defence improvements; and it provides the extra operational flexibility which is likely to be necessary as anti-submarine warfare techniques improve over the next twenty years.

Furthermore, it reverses a disadvantageous trend in the development of our nuclear striking force. Each new system since the bomber – Polaris in its original mode and subsequently Chevaline – has actually *reduced* the number of targets at which we can strike. Trident D5 significantly increases that number.

It seems clear, in cold logic, that the policy of the present government in basing its defence policies upon the foundation of effective nuclear deterrence is sound and prudent. In matters concerning nuclear weapons, however, logic is often driven out by emotion – especially by that most powerful of all emotions – fear. It is fear of the nuclear 'holocaust', rather than a more general revulsion against war, which has fuelled the current intensive phase in the pressure for arms control and disarmament. Yet this pressure springs from real and genuine concerns, a fact which must be recognized by any democratically elected government. Effective defence policies must therefore go hand in hand with the pursuit of balanced, multilateral and verifiable arms control agreements. It is *war* which we seek to avoid, not simply nuclear war.

One of the fallacies at the heart of the almost universal fear of nuclear weapons is the belief, carefully fostered by the 'peace movements', that we are on the brink of an apocalyptic disaster, which will lay waste to the world, annihilate its inhabitants in millions and bequeath to the future generations a legacy of mental and physical disease. That is certainly what would happen in a major nuclear war; but the danger of a war involving the great powers is probably less now than it has been on many occasions before the nuclear weapon was invented. The evidence of history is that arms races alone do not cause wars. The causes of war are subtle and intricate; they derive from political, economic and even psychological forces which eventually lead a power or group of powers to calculate that by using its military strength it can achieve gains which will outweigh the costs of war.

So far as the major armed confrontation in the world today is concerned – that between the Soviet Union and its allies on the one hand, and the Western Alliance on the other – the advent of nuclear weapons has profoundly and irrevocably altered the calculus. There is *no* political prize which either side could intelligently regard as being worth the risk of a nuclear war. Now that the great powers have the capacity to inflict intolerable damage and suffering upon each other, *and as long as each side knows that the other possesses that power*, the possibility of war between them is, in fact, remote. This will continue to be the case even if effective strategic defence systems are evolved.

This is not to suggest that the situation is therefore either desirable or permanently acceptable. Madmen have risen to positions of absolute power before, and they may do so again; the significance of the current uneasy confrontation is that, if the superpowers were plunged into a war, the consequences for the rest of the world would be almost un-imaginably dreadful – partly because they have amassed a stockpile of weapons with such potential for destruction that few people, any-where, would escape the effects entirely. The problem which we face, therefore, is how to reduce those stockpiles to a level at which the capacity to deter a potential enemy from going to war remains, without posing the threat of global disaster if the deterrent should ever fail.

In the past, then, the function of nuclear weapons has been as a mutually cancelling deterrent, maintained solely to insure each side against attack by the other. This situation was known variously as 'the balance of terror', 'the nuclear stalemate' or, by strategic analysts, as 'mutual assured destruction'.

With the emergence of new weapons of great accuracy and pene-trative power, strategic theorists have begun to discuss the possibility of 'disarming strikes' in which nuclear missiles would be used not to threaten the indiscriminate destruction of the enemy's cities, but to destroy his capacity to retaliate. Thus it is sometimes suggested that a nuclear war might now be 'winnable'. Variations on this theme include speculation about the possibility of a 'limited' nuclear war, in which an exchange of nuclear weapons between adversaries might be restricted as to their number, type or the geographical area in which they were used.

One of the results of this strange excursion into fantasy has been to exacerbate the natural feat of nuclear war and to provide a powerful impetus to anti-war and anti-nuclear protest movements in the West. Meanwhile, however, the built-in momentum of nuclear weapons development continues. Since late 1981, the Soviet Union has begun test flights of two new land-based intercontinental ballistic missiles, a new generation of strategic manned bombers and a new series of cruise missiles. President Reagan has authorized the deployment of a new intercontinental system – MX – and the United States has, at the request of its allies, deployed cruise missiles and a new generation of intermediate-range ballistic missiles in Western Europe. It is these missiles which are now the subject of arms control negotiations between the United States and the Soviet Union.

This constant accretion of nuclear weapons by the existing nuclear powers – sometimes referred to as 'vertical proliferation' – is now in danger of being matched by the development of 'horizontal proliferation' – the spread of nuclear weapons outside the five major powers which now possess them.

In an attempt to eliminate the obvious dangers of horizontal proliferation, a treaty was concluded in 1967 and subsequently signed and ratified by more than a hundred states. Under the terms of the Nuclear Non-Proliferation Treaty, nuclear weapon states agree not to transfer, and non-nuclear weapon states not to receive, nuclear weapons or the technology for their manufacture. The Non-Proliferation Treaty is only one example of the numerous attempts which have been made to control the power of the nuclear weapon since it made its first appearances at Hiroshima and Nagasaki. As early as 1946, the United States government put forward the Baruch Plan for the establishment of an international authority to control all atomic fuel and facilities and to supervise the destruction of all nuclear weapons. The Soviet Union rejected the Baruch Plan and put forward one of its own which was rejected by the United States on the grounds that it made inadequate provision for international inspection – an issue, incidentally, which has bedevilled arms control negotiations ever since. In 1959 the Antarctic Treaty prohibited all military and nuclear activities in the area; in 1963 the Partial Nuclear Test Ban Treaty banned the testing of nuclear weapons in space, in the atmosphere and underwater (but not underground); in 1967 a treaty was signed prohibiting the stationing of missiles in outer space; and in 1971 the positioning of nuclear devices on the seabed was forbidden.

In 1971 the first of the Strategic Arms Limitation agreements (SALT I) sought, without great success, to place limits on both the offensive and defensive nuclear missile systems of the United States and the Soviet Union. In 1974 the two superpowers agreed to the cessation of underground nuclear tests above a yield of 150 kilotons (the equivalent of 150,000 tons of high explosive); and in 1979 a second Strategic Arms Limitation Treaty (SALT II) made another attempt to limit American and Russian delivery systems. It has, however, never been ratified; it has been repeatedly contravened by the Soviet Union; and it has now been, for all practical purposes, renounced by the United States.

Whatever might be the value of these various agreements (and it is certainly greater than radical disarmament movements suggest), they suffer from two major weaknesses. The first is that they have never been universal in their application. Two of the five nuclear powers (France and China) have taken no part in the negotiations and are not formally bound by the treaties. The second is that no provision has been made for actual *disarmament* – for the reduction of existing levels of nuclear weapons. This has now become a matter of great urgency.

Although the 'numbers game' – the attempt to judge the nuclear balance on a numerical basis – is academic, and, in the context of the massive destructive power on both sides, largely irrelevant, a continuing competition in nuclear weapons contains a number of inherent dangers. In the first place, it distorts national economies by diverting valuable technological and human resources; secondly, it perpetuates a situation in which mechanical accident or gross political misjudgment could have catastrophic consequences; and, most important of all, an upward spiral of nuclear weapons development poses the threat that, at some stage, one side or the other may perceive that it has 'superiority', or that the other side might be about to achieve it – the 'window of vulnerability' theory. At such a stage the danger of a surprise or 'pre-emptive' attack is substantially increased.

A new and equally destabilizing factor has been introduced into the equation by the recent growth in the West of radical protest movements demanding one-sided disarmament and the dismantling of the Western Alliance. The inescapable consequence of what they are demanding would be to make nuclear war more, rather than less, likely. An uncontrolled, unbalanced *downward* spiral of disarmament would create the same dangerous instabilities as an uncontrolled upward spiral. Furthermore, unilateral disarmament by the West would clearly remove any modest incentive which at present exists for the Soviet Union to engage in binding international agreements.

International agreements on arms control – especially those concluded by the superpowers alone – should not, in any case, be regarded axiomatically as desirable. The current arms control dialogue between the United States and the Soviet Union provides a vivid example of the dangers and complications which arise from concentrating exclusively on a single category of weapons, instead of treating arms control as an integral element of defence policy as a whole. It must surely be obvious that arms control agreements are desirable only if they either reduce the level of the military threat, or increase the capability of the West to deal with it – or both. The proposal now being discussed between the superpowers would involve the removal from Europe of all Russian SS20 missiles, and all American cruise and Pershing missiles. Many military experts believe that this so-called 'zero option' contains a number of serious risks.

If, for example, the intermediate-range missiles were not to be dismantled, but simply moved out of Europe, the American cruise and Pershing would go back to the United States; the Russian SS20s might well be withdrawn east of the Ural Mountains, from where their 3000-mile range would still enable them to strike at almost any target in the NATO area. If the agreement were to dismantle the missiles, there would have to be a foolproof inspection system to guard against any possibility of cheating.

What worries NATO military commanders even more, however, is the threat which would be posed by shorter range nuclear missiles, in which the Soviet Union has built up a substantial lead since the cruise and Pershing missiles were deployed in Europe. The present negotiations on intermediate-range nuclear missiles do not affect missiles with ranges of less than 300 or more than 1200 miles. Many powerful Soviet missiles have a shorter range, and of these the weapon which causes greatest concern is the Scud, a mobile nuclear rocket with a range of nearly 200 miles. All the Warsaw Pact countries are equipped with these weapons, and more than 500 of them face the NATO forces with a stockpile of 2600 one-kiloton nuclear warheads, capable even from their peacetime locations of destroying targets in most of the Federal Republic of Germany.

As well as being able to deliver nuclear strikes, the Scud can be used with chemical warheads. The Soviet Union has the world's largest stockpile of chemical warfare agents, including nerve gases and blood agents such as hydrogen cyanide. Almost all Warsaw Pact conventional weapons systems are equipped with chemical ammunition, which could be used to contaminate airfields, depots and headquarters throughout most of West Germany. The Scud would be able to deliver its nerve-gas warheads well into the rear areas of the NATO military forces.

Furthermore the Scud will shortly be replaced by the SS23, a modern missile which will be capable of firing a 100-kiloton nuclear warhead (or a chemical weapon) over a range of 300 miles. This would bring targets in Belgium, the Netherlands and France within range, from the very first hours of a Soviet attack, from a weapon which is at present *not* included in any proposals for intermediate-range arms control.

The West, under such an arms control agreement, would be able to pose no comparable threat to the Warsaw Pact. With cruise and Pershing removed, the only nuclear weapons left would be very short-range artillery together with Lance missiles (maximum range about seventy miles) and F111 and Tornado aircraft, against which the Warsaw Pact has formidably effective anti-aircraft defences.

In these circumstances, it would not be possible to put into effect the NATO doctrine of flexible response. This involves meeting an enemy threat at enemy level, thereby reducing the danger of an all-out nuclear war. Apart from being unable to match the Warsaw Pact's nuclear and chemical threat, NATO would be unable to offer an effective conventional defence.

Great efforts have been made by the Soviet disinformation experts, with the busy assistance of 'peace-loving' elements in the West, to cast doubt on the superiority of Warsaw Pact conventional forces. The truth is that not only does the Pact have a clear advantage over NATO in almost every important military sense; more serious is that the situation has deteriorated over recent years, and continues to do so. Even in peacetime, the Warsaw Pact outnumbers NATO in troops, armoured divisions, main battle tanks, anti-tank guns, artillery and combat aircraft. Since 1974 the Warsaw Pact strength in main battle tanks has increased from just over 30,000 to nearly 46,000; and in artillery and mortars from 20,000 to 40,000. In the same period NATO's strength has remained at less than 15,000 in both categories.

In the event of war, the situation would quickly become even more serious, since the Soviet Union has quick, reasonably secure internal lines of communication along which to rush reserves and reinforcements. Most of NATO's reinforcements would have to come from the United States along extended and very vulnerable routes. When both NATO and the Warsaw Pact were fully reinforced in time of crisis or war, Allied Supreme Headquarters estimate that the Pact would have overwhelming superiority in every aspect of military strength.

There is, however, even greater cause for concern. Not only are NATO's conventional forces badly outnumbered; they are almost certainly less effective than those of the Warsaw Pact. In peacetime many of them are stationed far from their operational areas; indeed, some would have difficulty in reaching their defensive positions before the enemy. There are severe shortages of ammunition and fuel for training; equipment stocks are dangerously low and certainly would not be adequate for prolonged operations; there is a shortage of operational reserves and trained replacements for battle casualties.

The conclusion from all this is that if NATO were unable, by posing the threat of nuclear retaliation, to deter the Warsaw Pact from a conventional attack, the capacity of the West to defend itself against such an attack would be very limited. If this situation arose, the Soviet Union would not even have to mount such an attack. Its foreign policy aims in Europe could be achieved without firing a single shot.

These problems cannot be easily solved. Yet a number of general conclusions may be drawn. The first is that any form of unilateral disarmament, such as the removal of cruise and Pershing without any matching move by the Soviet Union, would be disastrous.

However, even if their removal were proposed as part of an agreement between the United States and the Soviet Union, there are a number of essential requirements which such an agreement should meet. First, the missiles concerned must be destroyed, not simply withdrawn. Secondly, their destruction must be fully and effectively inspected; thirdly, the treaty must include an agreement on shorter range nuclear missiles; and finally, no nuclear arms control agreements should be made in isolation from negotiations on the balanced reduction of conventional forces.

It is important, of course, that military commanders and advisers should understand the political arguments for effective and verifiable arms control agreements. At the same time political leaders must take seriously the concerns of their military advisers about the dangers which are inseparable from any change in the balance of forces.

An agreement on intermediate-range missiles is not only desirable in the long term; it is probably also inevitable. Both President Reagan and Mr Gorbachev have powerful incentives to reach such an agreement. European political leaders should therefore exercise their influence to ensure that agreement is not reached at all costs. Mrs Thatcher has already expressed concerns on this score and she should continue to do so, however loudly her critics may protest that she is 'torpedoing' the chances of arms control.

The West, as a whole, including President Reagan, has to understand that there is a price to be paid for nuclear arms control agreements. It will have to be paid principally to rescue our conventional defences from their present state of disrepair. This may mean additional expenditure on defence, a move which may be politically unwelcome, but which has to be approached realistically. For many years Western defence has depended on nuclear deterrence, which has prevented an open military conflict between East and West. If that posture is to be undermined by a process of nuclear disarmament, then it will be necessary to be able to defend ourselves effectively with non-nuclear forces.

The requirements in the European theatre of operations are fairly obvious. It is not necessary to increase the numbers of NATO forces substantially. It is necessary to ensure that they are well trained and well equipped. If they are not, not only will they be ineffective in war, they will be demoralized in peacetime. Senior British officers are already worried about the morale of the British Army of the Rhine, and it is essential that spares, ammunition, fuel and equipment should be available for training as well as for combat. It is important, too, that NATO's conventional forces should be able to attack enemy follow-up forces *before* they cross the River Elbe into West Germany. This will require fast, accurate intelligence and communications, using modern computer technology. It will also require highly accurate, destructive *non-nuclear* anti-armour missiles designed to destroy enemy armoured divisions without resorting to nuclear attack.

Finally, NATO troops must be in a position to deter the Warsaw Pact from using its massive chemical warfare potential. In an assault on Western Europe, the attacking forces would need to begin their attack with only *one* nerve gas shell on each of the defending formations to force all NATO's troops into their 'noddy-suits' – the cumbersome and clumsy anti-gas equipment which cuts down mobility, affects accuracy of shooting, and generally speaking substantially reduces the morale and efficiency of the defending forces.

What is needed is a clearly demonstrated ability by NATO to use its own chemical weapons at least until there is a verifiable international agreement banning the manufacture of chemical weapons altogether. Ideally these should be stationed in the European theatre. The 'binary' weapon, which keeps the missile and its chemical charge separate until the last moment, makes for safe handling and storage. Wherever the weapons are stationed, however, the Warsaw Pact should be confronted with the possibility that if they used chemical weapons, NATO would be able to retaliate in kind. At present only nuclear weapons are available as a retaliatory threat.

All this demands a much higher level of military cooperation among the European members of NATO. The present position is one of duplication, wasted resources, uncoordinated tactics and confused strategic doctrines. Those governments which support, for understandable political reasons, measures of nuclear disarmament simply have to face the need to provide the alternative military defences. This cannot be done on a piecemeal, nation-by-nation basis. It will, of course, need the support of the people of Western Europe. The governments of NATO's European nations have so far failed to convince their people of the serious, continuing nature of the Soviet threat. Indeed, beguiled by Mr Gorbachev's genial diplomacy, they seem to be even less convinced than ever.

CONCLUSION

The precarious and dangerous new strategic world into which Europe is moving presents the British government with a special challenge. Much has been done in recent years to improve the conditions in our armed forces; but a great deal more will be necessary in the dangerous years ahead. The Falklands factor, five years on, is beginning to fade. The Labour Party has adopted the dangerous, defeatist option of unilateral disarmament; the Alliance of SDP and Liberals seems undecided and confused about its defence policy.

The government must now demonstrate that in a changing international climate, in which the superpowers may come to significant agreements over the heads of Europe, it can adjust itself to the need for defence arrangements which will depend less and less on the American nuclear guarantee. This involves not only a robust and unshakeable attitude to Britain's own nuclear deterrent, but also an urgent programme to ensure that our conventional armed forces are of the highest calibre, and a determination to take the lead in promoting military cooperation in Western Europe.

It is important to recognize, furthermore, the great importance of the shift of emphasis in American strategic perceptions. United States foreign policy has rested securely for the last thirty years on the assumption that, to use a somewhat melodramatic conceit, the River Elbe is one of the frontiers of the United States. In other words, there has been an almost unchallenged consensus that one of the critical areas of American security lies in Europe and the Atlantic. It is upon this foundation that the North Atlantic Treaty Organization is built, it is for this reason that the United States keeps 300,000 troops in Germany, partly as an element of conventional military defence, but mainly as a 'hostage force' to demonstrate the validity of the American nuclear guarantee.

In recent years much has happened to cast doubts upon this central set of assumptions. Many percipient observers, for example, decline to endorse the credibility of 'extended deterrence', and question the validity of the theory of the American nuclear umbrella. Furthermore, the Soviet threat has long since ceased to be exclusively a matter of the red hordes pouring through France and Germany 'down to the Channel ports'. Vietnam, Afghanistan, Yemen, the Horn of Africa and Angola have demonstrated the global reach of Russian foreign policy; and the latest development is the emergence of a pattern of communist penetration in Latin America. For many Americans, events in Nicaragua and El Salvador are seen as the early warnings of a political transformation which might eventually pose a direct threat to the security of the southern United States. One American reaction to this perception might well be a demand for the withdrawal of American forces from Europe – a 'bring-the-boys-home' movement which, however precarious may be its basis in military logic, has a powerful emotive appeal. At a more sophisticated level the concept of 'global unilateralism' is already gaining in strength. In essence, this postulates an American foreign policy liberated from entangling and institutionalized alliances, free to seek its friends and allies pragmatically and to construct security policies with more apparent relevance to the global nature of the threat. It is a modified form of isolationism which would not necessarily exclude defence arrangements with *some* Western European countries, but which would almost certainly signal the end of the North Atlantic Treaty Organization in its present form.

If that happens, of course, one of the cardinal aims of Soviet foreign policy will have been achieved. It is a sterile exercise to engage in a debate about whether Russian policies are governed by a flexible opportunism. The dangers for the free world are the same in either case. What is clear beyond any reasonable doubt is that Russian long-term aims contain a number of identifiable elements. One of these is to bring about the disintegration of NATO and the separation of

Western Europe from the United States as a necessary prelude to the Finlandization of Western Europe.

The Soviet Union therefore has good reason to be pleased with what has happened to the West since the Second World War; the rise of neutralism and anti-Americanism in Western Europe has an especially piquant flavour when considered in the context of the continuing confrontation between the world's two principal political, ideological and economic groupings. The Soviet Union is a police state controlled by a totalitarian dictatorship; denial of human rights is institutionalized and any sign of dissent is brutally suppressed. Freedom, to generations of Russians, has been, and still is, an alien concept. These propositions may seem self-evident – they describe, indeed, the distinctive characteristics of any society which attempts to elevate the intellectual bankruptcy and moral squalor of Marxism into a political system. Yet it is necessary to insist upon them because the Soviet Union openly declares its desire to impose this system on the rest of the world, and has consistently demonstrated that it is prepared, if it seems necessary and feasible, to use force to do so.

There are, therefore, some simple facts to face. If the Western Alliance continues to disintegrate; and if the United States retreats into a carapace of 'global unilateralism', withdrawing its military presence from Europe and engaging in a bilateral relationship with the Soviet Union, the countries of Western Europe will have some hard choices to make, and they are not difficult to identify. One school of thought is being heard increasingly throughout the European Community – not only on the left of the political spectrum. Its dream is of some kind of Festung Europa, a Europe often in conflict with the United States, but in some mysterious way compatible with the wider community of the West. The concept is disturbingly fragile. There has been no evidence so far that Western Europe is capable even of harmonizing and coordinating its foreign policies, much less of forming any kind of political grouping strong enough to ensure its own security against military attack.

There is, of course, another option open to the countries of Western Europe. It is, put in its crudest form, to exchange dependence on the

United States for dependence on the Soviet Union – for this, as the Finnish position demonstrates, is one of the risks of neutrality. For those convinced of the pacific intentions of the Soviet Union, this course holds no terrors; there should be no doubt that if the North Atlantic Treaty Organization disintegrates into a collection of 'neutralist' nation states, denuded of credible deterrence or effective defence (and this is the logical conclusion of the policies advocated by the 'peace movements'), then their survival as free and independent societies will depend upon the whim of the Soviet Union. It is a course which has little attraction for those who are disposed to take the words and actions of the Russian leadership at their face value.

There is, in effect, no real choice for Western Europe. The inescapable necessity is to bend the efforts of foreign policy to repairing the cracks which are appearing in the Western Alliance; to recognize that there are long-term strategic concerns which override short- and medium-term conflicts of economic interests, because they are not matters simply of stability and prosperity but of survival. One of the cardinal aims of the Western European foreign policy should be to ensure that the United States remains fully engaged in the security of the free world. An essential prerequisite is to counter the insidious anti-Americanism which is, to the delight of our enemies, poisoning the mainstream of the Western Alliance.

The great question for the West now is whether the advance of Soviet imperialism has gone too far. The West has largely wasted the years since Suez; it can be argued that the free world should have marched against totalitarianism and authoritarianism wherever it appeared. It has been suggested that the central weakness of the West was that its biggest and most liberal state (the United States) failed to give a lead. Yet now that there are signs of a readiness in Washington to give that lead, the Alliance is still in disarray. Although its member states often share common values and attitudes towards the Marxist threat to a liberal world order, they tend to behave at times of crisis like hens in a thunderstorm, running in all directions with great speed but no common purpose. There is no coherent Western policy towards the Middle East, Central America, Africa, international terrorism,

Islamic fundamentalism or any of the problems which threaten the prosperity and survival of the free world. One of the principal sources of indecision and pusillanimity is the contemporary reluctance in the West to understand, as the Soviet Union understands very well, the significance of military power. Yet, for good or ill, that power is, and is likely to remain indefinitely, a decisive factor in determining the world order. The measured, deliberate application of military force, multiplied and reinforced by resolute political will, continues to be an indispensable element of policy. The paradox is that when there is a clear and unequivocal determination to use force in time, it may not be necessary at all. The Soviet Union understands this; there are depressing signs that the West does not.

NOTES

NOTES

1. V. I. Lenin, *Collected Works*, Vol. 29, pp. 138–9.
2. L. I. Brezhnev, *Pravda*, 22 December 1972.
3. V. Kortunov (member of staff of USSR Ministry of Foreign Affairs, 1968–73, and in 1984 assistant to the Chairman of Praesidium of the Supreme Soviet of USSR), *International Affairs*, no. 7, August 1974.
4. L. I. Brezhnev, *Pravda*, 13 November 1968.
5. A. A. Gromyko, *Africa and Asia Today*, July–August 1980.
6. I. B. Weydenthal *et al.*, *The Polish Drama 1980–82*, London 1983, pp. 111–12.
7. A. A. Gromyko, Report to USSR Supreme Soviet, 11 July 1969.
8. International Institute for Strategic Studies, *The Military Balance 1986–87*, London 1987, p. 36.
9. Editorial, *New Times*, January 1980.
10. L. I. Brezhnev, *Pravda*, 13 January 1980.
11. *Pravda*, 23 November 1956.
12. Tass, 21 August 1968.
13. Boris Dimitriyev, *Izvestia*, 10 August 1972.
14. L. I. Brezhnev, 'Letter of Thanks', *Pravda*, 7 September 1973.
15. *Great Soviet Encyclopedia*, 3rd Edition, London 1976, Vol. 16, p. 625.
16. *Pravda*, 21 December 1967.
17. A. A. Gromyko, *The Lenin Course of Foreign Policy of the Soviet Union*, Moscow 1962, pp. 95–6.
18. A. A. Gromyko, 'V. I. Lenin and the Foreign Policy of the Soviet State', *The Communist*, no. 6, 1983.
19. *Scientific Communism, a Glossary*, Moscow 1969.
20. KGB official training manual, quoted in US Congressional Hearings 1980.
21. Anatoly Golitsyn, address to Conference on Soviet Disinformation, Paris 1984.
22. Brian Crozier, *Strategy of Survival*, London 1978, pp. 142 and 146.
23. Ibid., pp. 143–5.
24. Speech, 1920, *Selected Works*, Vol. 8, p. 297.
25. *Pravda*, 16 September 1969.
26. Quoted in Brian Barron, *KGB*, London 1974, p. 165.
27. For examples, see Ray S. Cline and Yonah Alexander, *Terrorism: the Soviet Connection*, New York 1984, pp. 58ff.
28. V. Sokolovsky, *Military Strategy*, Moscow 1968.
29. Maj.-Gen. A. S. Milovidov, *The*

Philosophical Heritage of V. I. Lenin and Problems of Contemporary War, Moscow 1972, pp. 16–17.

30. Col. M. P. Skirdo, *The People, the Army, the Commander*, Moscow 1973, p. 78.

31. Gen. V. G. Kulikov (full member of the Central Committee of the CPSU; subsequently First Deputy Minister of Defence; Commander in Chief, Warsaw Pact Joint Forces; Marshal of USSR), *Pravda*, 13 November 1974.

32. Col. S. Tyushkevich, *Communist of the Armed Forces*, November 1975.

33. Senator Henry Jackson, First Jonathan Institute Conference on Terrorism, Jerusalem 1979.

34. Proceedings of the First Jonathan Institute Conference on Terrorism, Jerusalem 1979.

35. Ray S. Cline and Yonah Alexander, *op. cit.*

36. Claire Sterling, *The Terror Network*, London 1981.

37. Al Faji Al Jadid, March 1976.

38. Moamar al-Qaddafi, press conference, 2 May 1984.

39. Voice of the Arab Homeland, 22 April 1984.

40. *Terrorism and New Technologies of Destruction: an Overview of the Potential Risk*. A report for the National Advisory Committee Task Force on Disorder and Terrorism, BDM Corporation, 25 May 1976.

41. Professor J. B. Kelly, Second Jonathan Institute Conference on Terrorism, Washington 1984.

42. US Secretary of State George P. Shultz, Second Jonathan Institute Conference on Terrorism, Washington 1984.

43. Sir Kenneth Newman, 'Public Order in Free Societies', European Atlantic Group, London, 24 October 1983.

44. US Secretary of State George P. Shultz, Second Jonathan Institute Conference on Terrorism, Washington 1984.

45. Joseph M. Hassett, testimony on behalf of the American Civil Liberties Union before the Subcommittee on Security and Terrorism of the Senate Judiciary Committee, 6 June 1984.

46. Ibid.

47. *New York Times*, 31 October 1984.

48. Robert Kupperman, testimony before the Subcommittees on International Security and Scientific Affairs, and on International Operations, 7 June 1984.

49. Frank Brenchley, *Diplomatic Immunities and State-Sponsored Terrorism*, Institute for the Study of Conflict, London 1984.

50. Sir Geoffrey Jackson, Conference on Terrorism and the News Media, University of Aberdeen and the Centre for Contemporary Studies, May 1982; report published September 1983.

51. Jillian Becker, ibid.

52. Conference Report, *Political Communication and Persuasion*, Vol. 2, no. 3, New York 1984.

53. Coral Bell, *Strategic Thought in the Nuclear Age* (ed. Lawrence Martin), London 1979.

54. Alastair Buchan, *Crisis Management*, London 1964.

55. Kenneth Mackenzie, *Greece and*

Turkey: Disarray on Nato's Southern Flank, Institute for the Study of Conflict, London 1983.

56. Thanos Veremis, *Greek Security: Issues and Politics*, International Institute for Strategic Studies, London 1982.

57. Text of the North Atlantic Treaty, which entered into force on 24 August 1949, and to which Greece and Turkey acceded in February 1952.

58. Admiral W. J. Crowe Jr, *Nato's Sixteen Nations*, May–June 1983.

59. Duygu Bazoglu Sezer, *Turkey's Security Policies*, International Institute for Strategic Studies, London 1981.

60. Sergei G. Gorshkov, *Red Star Rising at Sea* (trans. Theodore A. Neely Jr), US Naval Institute, 1974.

61. Proceedings of the Spanish Cortes, 28 October 1981.

62. Brian Crozier, *The Surrogate Forces of the Soviet Union*, Institute for the Study of Conflict, London 1977.

63. David Lynn Price, *Morocco and the Sahara: Conflict and Development*, Institute for the Study of Conflict, London 1977.

64. Robert Olson, 'The Roots of Islam's Militancy', *Middle East International*, March 1984.

65. US Department of State Current

Policy Document No. 364, Bureau of Public Affairs, Washington, February 1982.

66. Jiri and Virginia Valenta, 'Soviet Strategy and Policies in the Caribbean Basin' in Howard J. Wiarde (ed.), *Rift and Revolution: The Central American Imbroglio*, Washington and London 1984.

67. Harold Blakemore, *Central American Crisis: Challenge to US Diplomacy*, Institute for the Study of Conflict, London 1985.

68. House of Commons, *Fifth Report from the Foreign Affairs Committee, Session 1981–82. Caribbean and Central America*, London 1982.

69. Jorge I. Dominguez, *US Interests and Policies in the Caribbean and Central America*, Washington and London 1982.

70. Lieut-General Heinz von zur Gathern, 'The Caribbean Basin and Global Strategy: Strategic Implications of the Soviet Moves in Central America on the NATO Alliance'. In report of a conference organized in Paris by the International Security Council, 17–22 February 1985.

71. British Government, *Statement on the Defence Estimates*, Part 11, 1985.

72. Roy Jenkins, *Afternoon on the Potomac?*, London 1972.

73. British Government, *Statement on the Defence Estimates*, Part 1, 1985.

INDEX